G-82/3   £4.50s

WITHDRAWN # SETTLEMENT GEOGRAPHY

CONCEPTS AND PROBLEMS

GEORGE GORDON M.A., Ph.D.
Senior Lecturer in Geography, University of Strathclyde

WILLIAM J. DICK B.A., Ph.D.
Principal Teacher of Geography, St. Modan's High School, Stirling

Designed and illustrated by Lewis Eadie

HOLMES McDOUGALL EDINBURGH

ACKNOWLEDGMENTS

For
Jane Gordon
and
Christine Dick.

First published 1982
© 1982 George Gordon and William Dick.

Published by
Holmes McDougall Ltd.,
Allander House,
137-141 Leith Walk,
Edinburgh EH6 8NS

The authors are indebted to many friends, colleagues and students, who helped to shape their ideas about Settlement Geography.

They are extremely indebted to Mrs M. MacLeod and Mrs J. Simpson, who typed most of the manuscript, Mr B. Reeves who reproduced the photographs and many of the maps and to Miss R. Spence who drew some of the maps. Sincere thanks are extended to Mr L. Eadie for the artwork and design, to Mrs T. Duriez, copy-editor, and to Mr I. McLean and Mr I. Christie, editors. Dr Dick is grateful to Miss E. Cairney, Miss A. Campbell and Miss P. Robertson for fieldwork assistance and to Mr W. F. O'Carroll for his help and encouragement.

The authors and publishers wish to acknowledge the many contributors of illustrations who have allowed copyright works to be reproduced: Aerofilms for Figs 1.8, 1.13, 1.16, 1.23, 2.13, 2.14, 2.23, 2.26, 2.27, 4.22, 4.23, 5.4, 5.5, 6.4b; American Academy of Political and Social Science with C. D. Harris for the diagram of the Multiple Nuclei Model on p. 13 of 'The nature of cities' by C. D. Harris and E. Ullman which appeared in *The Annals of the AAPSS*, vol. 242; American Geographical Society with C. D. Harris for Fig. 1 from *Geographical Review*, 33, 1943; Association of Japanese Geographers with Y. Masai for diagram of townscapes of the major cultural regions from 'The contemporary Japanese townscape' in *Japanese Cities: a Geographical approach*; Associated Press for Figs. 1.34, 5.24c; Bell & Hyman Publs. with T. T. McGee for the model of a Southeast Asian city from *The Southeast Asian City*; B & S Colour Lab. and Strathclyde Passenger Transport Executive for Fig. 5.15; British Tourist Authority for Fig. 1.10; Census volume and Registrar-General for data for Figs. 5.12a and b; Le Centre National de la Recherche Scientifique for the drawing of St Laurent-de-la Salanque p. 69 of *L'Atlas de France*; Countryside Commission for

England and Wales for use of map to form basis of Fig. 6.16; Croom Helm with I. H. Adams for Fig. 1.3 from *The Making of Urban Scotland; Festschrift Karl Sinnhuber* vol. II, with G. Gordon for Figs. 5.19 and 5.20 from 'Working-class housing in Edinburgh 1837-1974'; Forestry Commission for maps used as base for Fig. 6.18; Freeman Fox for map of underground system in Hong Kong; The Geographical Association for figure of the Urban Hierarchy, p. 43 of A. E. Smailes' article in *Geography*, 29, 1944; *Geographical Journal* with F. H. W. Green for map of urban hinterland in 'Urban hinterlands in England and Wales: an analysis of bus services', vol. CXV, 1950; *The Geographical Magazine* with M. Hillman and A. Whalley for the drawing which appeared in August, 1978 issue; George Philip & Son Ltd. with F. E. I. Hamilton for the model of the industrial structure of a city in J. E. Mailin, *A Geography of Greater London;* Greater London Development Plan Statement Fig. 5 used as base for Fig. 5.15; Harper & Row Publs. Inc. with G. J. Fielding for p. 166 from *Geography as a Social Science;* G. Hollier for Fig. 1.36; Hong Kong Government Office for Figs. 5.17b-c; Professor G. M. Howe for figure showing cancer of the lung and bronchus (female); Hutchinson & Co. Ltd. with W. Mead and E. Brown for Fig. 30 from *The United States and Canada;* Instituto de Credito Territorial, Colombia for Fig. 5.25; International Labour Office Geneva with H. Joshi, H. Lubell and J. Meuly for use of base map of Abidjan; Lawrence with D. Knos for diagram from *Distribution* of Land Values in Topeka; Leonard Hill and Publs. with F. Ossorn and A. Whittick for map of Crawley from New Towns; the Answer to Megalopolis; London Transport for underground map registered user No. 83/003; Longman Group Ltd. with J. A. Everson and B. P. Fitzgerald for Fig. 50 from *Settlement Patterns* and for Fig. 52, p. 67 from *Inside the City* and with J. Beaujeu-Garneier for Fig. 10, p. 87 from *France;* Macdonald & Evans with F. S. Hudson for Fig. 9.9 from *Geography of Settlements;* Iain McLean for Figs. 1.1b-e; The University of Chicago Press for Fig. 1.1, p. 4 from *The American City; Milngavie Herald* for Fig. 6.22; National Housing Bank Brazil for Figs. 4.13, 5.24a and b; Nelson & Sons Ltd. with R. W. Lawton for Figs. 29a and b from his chapter in J. W. Watson and J. B. Sissons, *The British Isles: A Systematic Geography;* Niedersächsisches Landesverwaltungsamt — Landesvermessung for extract of Borde sheet; Norwich Tourist Office for Fig. 4.12b; Oliver & Boyd with P. Daniel and M. Hopkinson for Fig. 4.17 from *The Geography of Settlement;* Ordnance Survey and the Controller of HMSO for extracts from 1:50 000 Malton sheet and for information from map of Cambridge, Isle of Ely and Snowdonia: Crown Copyright Reserved; Pergamon Press Ltd. with J. H. Johnson for Fig. 30 from *Urban Geography* and with P. Gould and R. White for maps of Bristol and Liverpool school-leavers from 'The mental maps of British school-leavers', *Regional Studies,* No. 2, 1968 and with J. B. Goddard for diagram from 'Multivariate analysis of office location patterns in a city centre: a London example', *Regional Studies,* vol. 2, 1968; Prentice Hall Inc. with B. Berry and F. Horton for Figs. 2.1 and 2.9 from *Geographic Perspectives on Urban Systems* which were based on material in *East Lakes Geographer,* vol. 2, *Studies in Geography Series* published by Department of Geography at Northwestern University and J. Borchert, *Geographical Review,* vol. 57, 1967 with permission of the American Geographical Society, University of Chicago, Department of Geography, Research Monograph, no. 92 with the Goode Base Map, and with B. Berry for Figs. 1.13, 1.15, 1.18, 2.1, 3.14, 3.15 from *Geography of Market Centres and Retail Distribution* (Figs. 3.14 and 3.15 from G. William Skinner, 'Marketing and Social Structure in Rural China', Journal of Asian Studies, vol. 24, Nos. 1-3); Presse und Informationsamt der Stadt Duisburg for Fig. 2.30; Proceedings of the International Study Week, Amsterdam with E. J. Brill, J. Goddard, W. J. Heinemeijer et al for figure from 'Urban core and inner city'; *Resources for the Future Inc.,* publs. The John Hopkins University Press with L. Wingo for Fig. 11 from *Transportation and Urban Land; Railway Gazette* for map of underground railway in Hong Kong; Rotterdam Port Authority and Aerophoto Schiphol for Fig. 2.29; Routledge & Kegan Paul with P. Mann for figure of the structure of a British city from *An approach to Urban Sociology;* J. Sallnow for Figs. 1.37, 4.48; Scottish Certificate of Education Examination Board; Scottish Development Department for Fig. 1.6; *Scottish Geographical Magazine* with D. G. Lockhart for plans from 'Scottish village plans: a preliminary analysis', vol. 96. No. 3 and with H. R. Jones for Fig. 1 from 'Migration in Scotland', vol. 83, No. 3, 1967; Second Land Utilisation Survey of Britain and Miss. A. Coleman; David Simister of Simister, Monaghan, McKinney for 5.12b; *Tijdschrift voor Economische en Sociale Geografie* with A. H. Dawson for figure of schematic plan of a socialist city from 'Warsaw: an example of city structure in free-market and planned socialist environments', vol. 62, 1971; Town and Country Planning, Nov. 1980 for British New Town data; Twentieth Century Funds Publs. for a drawing from J. Gottmann's *Megalopolis;* United Nations, New York, 1971, Report of Medellin Conference of 1970, Department of Economic and Social Affairs for material from 'Improvement of Slums and Uncontrolled Settlements'; United States Department of Internal Geological Survey for extract from Salt Lake City sheet and Monkato, Minnesota sheet; United States Government Printing Office with H. Hoyt for material from *The Structure and Growth of Residential Neighbourhoods in American Cities,* 1939; University of Cambridge, Committee for Aerial Photography for Fig. 1.7; University of Chicago Press with R. Park and E. Burgess for concentric model of urban structure and map of urban zones in Chicago, pp. 51-3 from *The City;* University of Washington Press with E. M. Horwood and R. R. Boyce for figure of core-frame model from *Studies in the Central Business District and Urban Freeway Development,* p. 75; Derek G. Widdicombe. The publishers also wish to thank George Gordon himself for Figs. 1.14, 1.15, 1.17, 1.18a and b, 1.20-22, 4.3a-d, 4.4, 4.11, 4.12a, 4.14-21, 4.33, 4.37, 4.38, 5.2, 5.3, 5.18, 5.21a, 6.11, 6.15.

The authors and publishers have made every effort to trace the copyright of the material used in this book, and in any case where they have been unsuccessful, apologize for any accidental infringement of copyright.

CONTENTS

Fig. 1:1a
Central London.

Fig. 1:b Swanston village near Edinburgh.

Fig. 1:1d Newtongrange: A Midlothian mining settlement.

Fig. 1:1c A Farm in Southern Scotland.

Fig. 1:1e City meets country on the southern edge of Edinburgh.

CHAPTER ONE
INTRODUCTION

What do we mean by the word **settlement**? Do you immediately think of the noise and bustle of a major city such as London (Fig. 1:1a)? The honking of horns, the clicking of typewriters in the numerous blocks of offices, the jostling crowds of shoppers in Oxford Street and Kensington High Street are all images of a major city or a metropolis. Or perhaps you visualize a village clustered around a green, a church or a crossroads (Fig. 1:1b) — a neatly **structured settlement** with a clear focus. Compared to the metropolis, the village seems simpler, more peaceful, almost sleepy. Yet it has a part to play in the life of our society. It performs certain functions for the residents of the village and the surrounding area; functions such as shops, schools, and medical services. What about the pattern shown in Fig. 1:1c? Is that an example of settlement? Well, if we define settlement as a permanent place of residence of people, then farms are a form of settlement although the bleating of sheep or the lowing of cattle may seem in total contrast to the image of urban settlements, the image of towns and cities. Certainly a group of farms in a hamlet forms a settlement. But we also talk about a pattern of farms dotted about the countryside as **dispersed settlement**. Here each farm is isolated but, in total, they form a type of spaced out settlement.

Whatever the type of settlements the buildings have a particular role or **function**. On the farm one type of building is suited to the role of milking-parlour but another structure would be required for a hay barn. Equally in towns and cities we have specialized buildings such as offices, shops, schools, discos, hotels, law courts, churches, factories and warehouses.

Two more examples add different images of settlements. First, in Fig. 1:1d, the distinctive landscape of a mining village with the symbols of the industry, the pithead winding machinery and the spoil heaps and streets of houses, which seem urban in character. Yet most mining villages are not parts of cities but are located outside the main cities and towns. If we make a simple distinction between town and country, then mining villages are located in the country but the economic activity (mining) is more associated with the industrial functions in towns and cities. Second, as major cities and towns grow new housing areas invade the countryside (Fig. 1:1e). These areas of suburban housing often lack a central **focus** such as the cross or green in a village. They are rather amorphous extensions of the city rather than distinct and separate settlements, a part of a larger pattern rather than a separate type of settlement.

From these pictures we can suggest a number of features which can be used to define types of settlements. For example, we can use features such as population size, function, physical character and economic activity. These features are examined in detail in Chapter 2.

The number of residents is a simple method of classifying settlements into broad categories such as hamlet, village, town, city, metropolis and megalopolis. The population figures are provided by national censuses which are taken at various times, e.g. every ten years in Britain. In most cases the census determines some decisions about settlements because a particular size is required before the statistics for a settlement are listed separately. For example, in Denmark places with more than 200 residents are listed as towns, but in

Greece a town must have at least 10 000 inhabitants. The smaller settlements will be added together with farms and shown as a district total which represents a number of settlements ranging from isolated farms to substantial villages.

Urban and Rural Settlements

We can group settlements into two major types, urban and rural. On the basis of size a simple guideline would be that settlements smaller than towns were rural and those the size of, or larger than, a town, urban. But as we have seen that definition can range from 200 to 10 000 people as the dividing line between rural and urban settlements. Rural settlements are associated with the land and activities such as farming, fishing and forestry whereas urban centres are inhabited by people engaged in manufacturing and service activities (shops and offices). This apparently simple distinction is often complex in reality. Second-home ownership in quiet rural areas of Britain illustrates the invasion of rural settlements by urban dwellers. Equally in developing countries such as India settlements with well over 20 000 people can have more than half of the population engaged in farming. Farming can result in a dispersed pattern of individual farms but it can be organized from focal points such as villages and towns. Much depends upon the type of farming, the average size of the farm and the intensity and scale of cultivation. Similarly, the invasion of rural areas in developed countries such as Britain or America by commuters or second-home owners illustrates the effects of transport improvements in the twentieth century, particularly the motor car.

Urbanization

This involves an increase in the percentage of the population of a country living in urban settlements. On the world scale about two in every five people live in urban settlements but this average figure conceals wide variations. In Britain probably more than 80 per cent of the population

should be classed as urban dwellers, whereas in many African countries more than half of the people live in the countryside. To a considerable extent these differences reflect the historical development of the countries. Those countries which led the Industrial Revolution in the nineteenth century have reached a high level of urbanization. By contrast, the less developed countries are now experiencing rapid urbanization as illustrated by the rapid growth of cities such as Calcutta.

Fig. 1:2 shows the net movement between different types of settlement in Scotland in 1960 to 1961. Remember it is the net movement. For example, people did move from landward areas to small burghs but far more moved in the opposite direction, producing the largest flow shown in the diagram. The landward areas include both rural areas and rural-urban areas. The latter consist of the fringe of commuter villages around the major cities and in a dispersed zone throughout much of Central Scotland.

In developing countries such as India a different pattern of migration is operating with the dominant flow being from landward areas to major cities, although there are movements of people to towns and small cities.

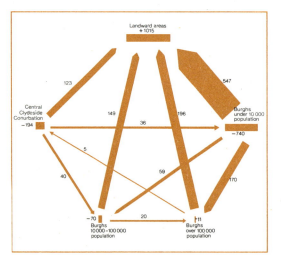

Fig. 1:2
Migration in Scotland in the early 1960s (H. JONES).

Assignments
1 With reference to Fig. 1:2 try to draw a schematic diagram of migration flows between types of settlement unit in India or any other developing country.
2 Fig. 1:2 does not identify New Towns as a category of settlement unit. How do you think that would modify the diagram?

Very Large Settlements

Three large settlement forms are recognized: (a) conurbation (b) metropolis (c) megalopolis.

A **conurbation** is a large built-up area produced when the growth of a city engulfs previously separate settlements to give a town within a city situation. The Clydeside Conurbation (Fig. 1:3) centred on Glasgow includes the towns such as Paisley, Clydebank, Renfrew and Rutherglen. The growth of Glasgow in the nineteenth and early twentieth centuries also led to the incorporation of independent industrial and suburban settlements such as Partick, Govan and Pollokshaws. The other principal British conurbations are Greater London, the West Midlands, the West Riding, South-East Lancashire, Merseyside and Tyneside, respectively centred upon London, Birmingham, Leeds, Manchester, Liverpool and Newcastle. The West Midlands conurbation embraces the 'Black Country', the urban and industrial region west and north-west of Birmingham including Wolverhampton and Stourbridge.

A **metropolis** is a very large and very important city such as London, Paris, New York or Tokyo. The term means more than a large population, it implies the great functional importance of that city in national and international trade, services and influence. The metropolis will be the centre of the media (newspapers and broadcasting), as well as the financial and business heart of the nation. Sometimes you will find the term applied to all large cities, perhaps of more than one million inhabitants, but many of these cities are major regional centres with limited international significance. In 1979 it was estimated that there were twenty-one settlements in China with more than one million inhabitants, fourteen in the U.S.S.R. and more than thirty in the U.S.A. At that time it was estimated that there were seventeen settlements in the world with more than five million inhabitants (Mexico City, Tokyo, New York, Shanghai, Paris, Buenos Aires, Moscow, Peking, Rio de Janeiro, Los Angeles, Calcutta, Chicago, London, Seoul, Sao Paulo, Cairo). Do we reserve the term metropolis for these settlements in the list above or apply it to all very large extended cities such as Greater Glasgow and Greater Manchester? Transport developments have allowed people to separate place of residence and place of work. This encouraged the growth of extensive urban areas around major cities which we try to capture in the name Greater London (Fig. 1:4) or Greater Glasgow, meaning a commuting zone around the city itself which will include farmland, open space and numerous villages and towns partly affected by the development of dormitory settlements, the houses of people who work in the city but live in the fringe zone around the city.

Megalopolis is a term coined to describe the settlement pattern where a number of large cities begin to meet forming a vast settled zone. It was first applied by Jean Gottmann to a 960 kilometre section on the north-east Seaboard of the United States stretching from Northern Virginia to New Hampshire (Fig. 1:5). At that time (1960) the area had a population of 37 millions and was characterized by the overlapping of commuting zones to major cities. This area is sometimes called Bosnywash (Boston, New York, Washington) and by 1975 to 1976 it contained about 44 million people. The term megalopolis has subsequently been applied to other very large shapeless complex urban regions such as the Lower Great Lakes area, the Los Angeles-San Francisco corridor, Greater Tokyo and, in Britain, the London-Liverpool axis.

The classification of types of settlements is not simply dependent upon size but also function and this topic is examined in greater detail in Chapter 2.

Fig. 1:3 The Clydeside Conurbation.

Fig. 1:4 Greater London.

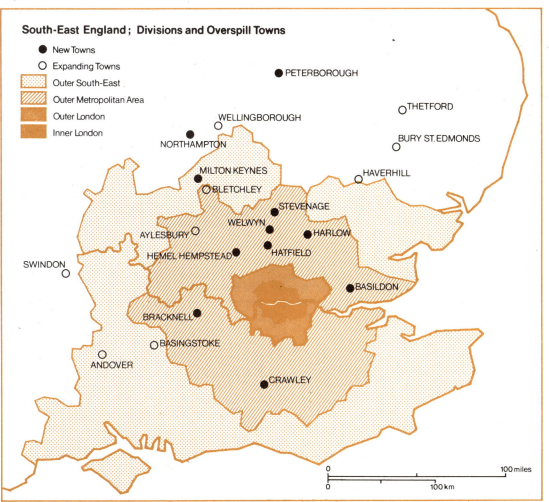

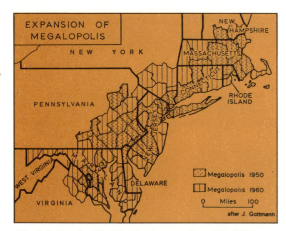

Fig. 1:5 Megalopolis: The North-east region of the USA.

Settlement Origins and Growth

Most settlements in Western Europe date from medieval times. The period between 1000 and 1500 AD established the basic settlement framework in many European countries, notably England, Wales and Scotland. Later a further layer of settlements was added during the Industrial Revolution. In Britain, these settlements were mainly associated with the location of the major coalfields. In the present century suburban growth, the creation of New Towns and the decline of some old industrial centres and the loss of population in the inner areas of major cities, have been important sources of change in the settlement pattern.

PRE-ROMAN SETTLEMENTS

Between about 4300 BC and the arrival of the Romans in Britain in 43 AD three major waves of settlement occurred, known as the Neolithic, the Bronze Age and the Iron Age because of the dominance of stone, bronze and iron implements in each period. The remains of the earliest phase, the Neolithic, are marked by long barrows and megalithic tombs. The small cluster of stone huts linked by covered passages at Scara Brae (Fig. 1:6) in Orkney may be the oldest settlement in Western Europe. Later Bronze and Iron Age set-

tlements were also small and isolated agricultural communities in which self-sufficiency demanded the practising of skills such as metal-working to make simple agricultural tools. Many early settlements were located on elevated sites, partly for defence but also to avoid wet, heavy soils. The inhabitants were pastoralists, animal-keepers, but they also cultivated small plots beside the settlements. The long and round barrows are burial chambers not the remains of houses but the traces of Iron Age hill-forts and brochs (bell-shaped towers) are more widespread evidence of actual settlements. The discovery of Bronze and Iron Age remains at Cairnpapple Hill near Linlithgow in Central Scotland suggests a continuity of settlement at that location for a prolonged period in pre-Roman times. Natural eminences

such as Cairnpapple Hill or Traprain Law (Fig. 1:7) in East Lothian attracted early settlement but Iron Age forts were located on the upper slopes of valleys within upland areas such as Edin's Broch on Cockburn Law in the Border Region. There were some six hundred hill-forts in England and Wales. These were mostly located in Southern England and Wales with a marked absence of forts in North and Eastern England. Settlements were sometimes built upon piles driven into the bed of a lake as at Glastonbury, Somerset. In Scotland these are called crannogs and evidence of such settlements has been found at several locations. Complex features date from this period such as the mysteriously vitrified Iron Age stone forts of Scotland and the elaborate earthworks at Maiden Castle, Dorset (Fig. 1:8).

Fig. 1:7
Traprain Law, East Lothian. The upstanding volcanic rock offered a defensive site for a community of local tribesmen during the period of the Roman occupation of Britain.

Fig. 1:6
Scara Brae, Orkney. Site of a Celtic settlement duating from around 2500 BC. The settlement consisted of a small group of huts.

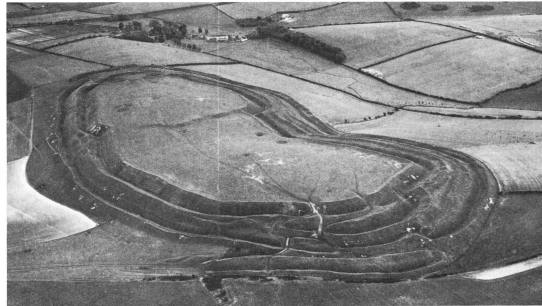

Fig. 1:8
Maiden Castle, Dorset. In this case earthworks and trenches provided a system of defence for this elevated early settlement.

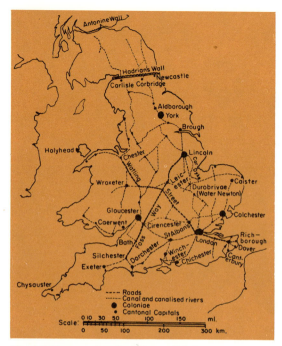
Fig. 1:9 Towns and roads of Roman Britain.

Fig. 1:10 Remains of a Roman villa, Chedworth, Cotswolds.

ROMAN SETTLEMENT

Fig. 1:9 summarizes the pattern of towns and roads in Roman Britain. Sections of Roman road are still in use today and many of the routes were closely followed by railway engineers in the nineteenth century seeking to avoid excessive gradients whilst searching for the shortest acceptable route between settlements. Some Roman settlements were based upon the sites of existing forts, others were new. London, a new settlement, was the principal town, with Gloucester, Lincoln, Colchester and York as the remaining major towns. The network of settlements, large and small, acted as administrative and military centres, controlling the trade and production of local areas. Large villas, such as Chedworth in the Cotswolds (Fig. 1:10) formed a distinctive element in the pattern of settlement. The villas organized manufacturing of cloth and agricultural production, although some, including Chedworth, were elaborate constructions which probably acted as recreational retreats for wealthy Romans. At Chedworth, which was located in a sheltered Cotswold valley or combe, thirty-two rooms have been identified. These include two bath suites, one akin to a modern Turkish bath and the other resembling a sauna. The site of this fourth-century A.D. villa is now preserved by The National Trust.

MEDIEVAL BRITAIN

The troubled six centuries following the departure of the Romans did not present ideal conditions for the establishment of settlements, particularly the founding and growth of towns. Place-names give some clues about geographical patterns during this period. In England Anglo-Saxon settlement is shown by the numerous place-names of Anglo-Saxon origin (see Fig. 1:11). The Saxons cleared woodland and created a village-based agricultural landscape. Villages stood around a green, with the strips of intensively cultivated land behind the houses. Many villages were linear in shape (known as **Strassendorf** in Central Europe) but some were circular. These green villages are found throughout lowland Britain from Durham to Devon, e.g.

Early settlements		Later growth period	
		Evidence of environmental factors	
Homestead or farmsteads	Offspring settlements	Wood clearing	Drainage settlements
- ing	cot; -cote (outlying village)	den; -dene (swine pasture)	eg; ey; ea; eig (island)
- ham			
- ton	croft (small enclosure)	hurst; hirst (coppice on a hill)	fen
			lake
- tun	stead (place)	holt (wood)	
			mere
- ingham	stow (holy place)	leaze; -lee; lea; -ley; leigh (clearing)	moss
- ington	wike; -wick; wick, wic (often a cattle farm)	riding; -rod (cleared land)	
		weald; -wold (wooded upland or grazing)	

Fig. 1:11 *Anglo-Saxon place-name endings (after A. GUEST).*

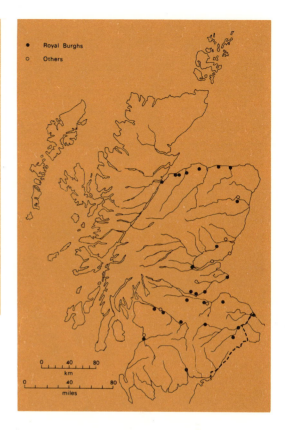

Fig. 1:12 *The distribution of burghs in medieval Scotland (I. H. ADAMS).*

Piercebridge, Durham or Finchingfield in Essex. Few examples occur in Scotland and most of those are located in East Lothian, e.g. Dirleton. Linear and circular villages probably existed before Anglo-Saxon times: for example, there were circular Celtic villages. The Anglo-Saxon period established the pattern of settlement for several centuries.

An extensive network of villages existed by the time of the Norman invasion of England in the eleventh century. The Normans brought a system of centralized government which required a system of boroughs or towns to control regions, organize trade and administer laws and the collection of taxes. In the twelfth century some thirty burghs were founded in Scotland which performed similar functions (Fig. 1:12). Notable amongst these royal burghs were Aberdeen, Berwick, Dundee, Edinburgh, Elgin, Haddington, Jedburgh, Lanark, Linlithgow and Stirling. Some of these settlements later became cities, others remained small, e.g. Crail.

Two further components of the settlement pattern in this period were castles and church properties. Many boroughs were fortified reflecting the troubled times of the medieval period. The walled bastide castle towns of Wales such as Conwy were particularly formal examples of this trend. There were ecclesiastical (church) burghs in Scotland, notably Glasgow and Dunfermline. In England settlements such as Canterbury and York were strongly influenced by their role as ecclesiastical centres. In addition monasteries were important centres of agricultural development and educational provision. The agricultural function had the greatest impact on the landscape with the monasteries amongst the leaders in the evolution of various forms of farming. Abbeys such as Melrose and Dryburgh in Southern Scotland and Fountains and Rievaulx in Yorkshire were major centres of comparatively large scale cereal production and sheep farming in an era of predominantly low yields and levels of output in British farming.

Assignment

3 In the medieval period Scotland had important trading links with countries around the Baltic Sea and also with the Low Countries and France. Transport was primarily water-borne, overland transport being limited to pack horses. Consider these points and, with reference to Fig. 1:12, attempt an explanation of the distribution of burghs in Norman times.

13

eight kilometres. In the towns specialists made and sold goods such as metal-ware. They became organized into guilds, groups of people practising a particular trade or craft. We can think of these as being both small workshop industries and shops selling the goods. The medieval town was dominated by the main street, the market place and the church. Narrow plots with houses and yards flanked this street and there were a number of minor lanes. In time some towns grew and extended across adjoining fields but the centre of many small market towns still retains the distinctive layout of the medieval period (Fig. 1:16).

SETTLEMENT EVOLUTION IN BRITAIN 1500-1800

Change did occur. Some towns grew, others declined. New settlements were started, often as a deliberate attempt by landowners to develop agriculture or industry. This was also the period when a more formal organization of towns became fashionable in Europe, particularly in France and Italy. A striking example was the creation of the Piazza di San Marco, St. Mark's Square, Venice (Fig. 1:17). By the end of the seventeenth century Paris was the most populated (more than half a million) and most important European capital. There were a number of large cities such as London, Lisbon, Amsterdam, Rome, Seville and Antwerp, which acted as national centres of administration and trade. (The relationship of settlements to their hinterlands is examined in greater depth in Chapter 3.)

New developments and ideas spread from these large cities to other settlements and other countries. This was an age of sharp contrasts of grandeur and squalor, the elegant squares and fine buildings contrasting with the hovels of the poor. Medical knowledge was limited, so disease and epidemics could kill thousands in the congested densely-packed houses of these cities.

At the start of this period society was much more violent. There were continual fears of mob insurrection, revolt by the nobility and the danger of foreign invasion. By 1800 there was a greater guarantee of stability with the introduction of a standing army after 1660 and revolt by the nobility no longer a threat. Also epidemic and endemic disease declined to some extent after 1665. The

Fig. 1:13 Conwy, North Wales. A fine example of a walled medieval Welsh town guarded by a fortress. The two road bridges and the railway bridge emphasise the strategic location of the fortress.

In Wales Edward I built several fortified settlements known as **bastides** such as Flint, Rhuddlan and Conwy (Fig. 1:13).

Most towns at this time were market towns focussed around the market square, market house (Fig. 1:14) or market cross as at Malmesbury (Fig. 1:15). They had a charter from the monarch which gave the town the right to hold markets both for local produce and for goods brought in from other places. The area served by the market town was limited to the distance villagers could cover in a day, approximately six to

Fig. 1:14 *The market house, Tetbury.*

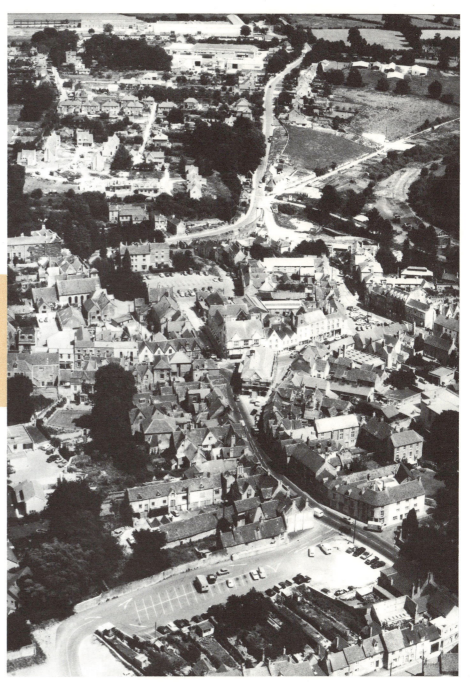

Fig. 1:16
The layout of a medieval market town, Tetbury, Cotswolds. The market house can be seen in the middle of the photograph. There is a marked valley between the market house and the modern housing at the top of the photograph.

Fig. 1:15 *The market cross, Malmesbury.*

Fig. 1:17 St. Mark's Square, Venice.

Fig. 1:18a The Circus, Bath.

Fig. 1:18b Royal Crescent, Bath.

time after the Civil War and Commonwealth therefore marked an important change. This was the age of the Renaissance, a rebirth of the culture and learning of ancient Greece and Rome. There were large-scale land development schemes of town housing in the middle of the seventeenth century. Covent Garden Square, built in 1631, Leicester Square in 1635 and Bloomsbury Square in 1665, adopted the architectural fashion of the Renaissance period with substantial terraced houses arranged around a large garden. This was carried still further by architects like Christopher Wren, Nicholas Hawksmoor and John Vanburgh following the devastation of the Great Fire of London in 1666. Soho Square was built in 1681, Grosvenor Square in 1695 and Berkeley Square in 1698 (although the façades and uses to which these buildings have been put have changed con-

siderably over the years). Large projects reflecting this style were built in Edinburgh and Bath during the eighteenth century and many small towns had one square built in this manner.

At Bath, Beau Nash and two associates created an elegant district of terraced houses on the sloping ground overlooking the medieval core. The town had become a popular health resort because of the medical properties of the spa waters. Wealthy people bought or rented the new town houses for their seasonal visit to take the waters. The Circus (Fig. 1:18a) and Royal Crescent (Fig. 1:18b) are notable examples of these developments dating from the 1760s and 1770s. At the same time in Edinburgh a new town for the wealthy was started on a site to the north of the old medieval core. The plan (Fig. 1:19) consisted of three main streets (Princes Street, George Street and Queen

Street) and two Squares (Charlotte Square and St. Andrew's Square). The large terraced mansions in the principal thoroughfares contrasted with the small tradesmen's flats in minor streets such as Rose Street.

Opposite – Fig. 1:19
Plan of the 18th century New Town of Edinburgh.

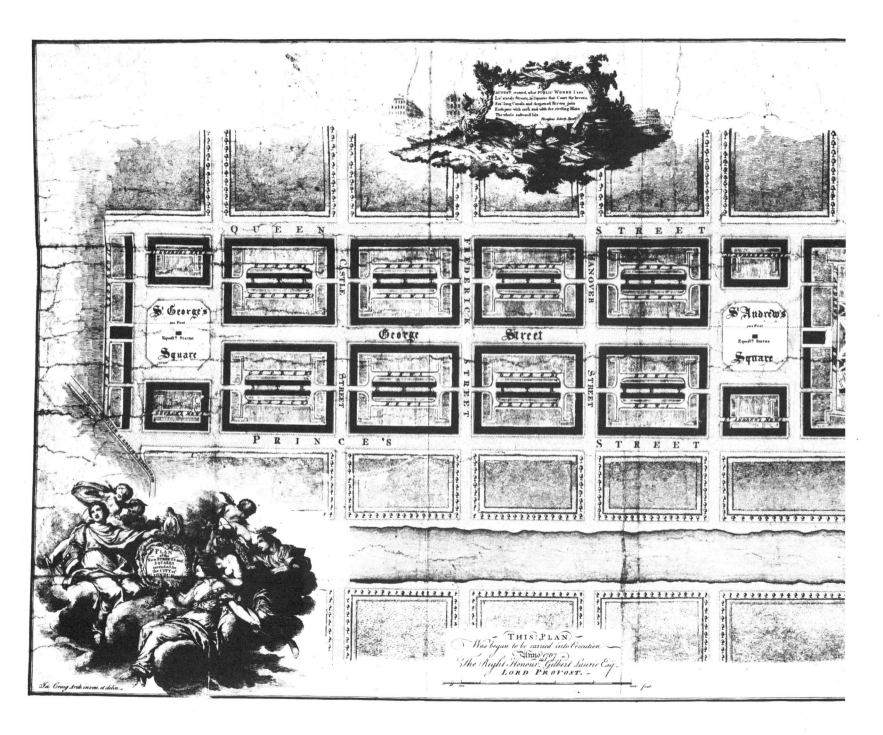

QUEEN   STREET

St George's
100 Feet

Equest. Statue

Square

George   Street

PRINCE'S   STREET

St Andrew's
100 Feet

Equest. Statue

Square

PLAN
of the
New STREETS and
SQUARES
intended for
the CITY of
DUBLIN

Ja: Craig Arch. inven. et delin.

THIS PLAN
Was begun to be carried into Execution
Anno 1767
The Right Honour. Gilbert Laurie Esq.
LORD PROVOST.

17

Fig. 1:20 *Conversion of original houses to offices, George Street, Edinburgh.*

Fig. 1:21 *Replacement of the original ground floor exterior by a new office frontage, George Street, Edinburgh.*

Fig. 1:22 *Some Georgian houses in Edinburgh are still used as houses.*

Many of the seventeenth- and eighteenth-century mansions have been converted into shops or offices (Fig. 1:20), or replaced by new buildings designed for offices or shops (Fig. 1:21) but some are still used as houses (Fig. 1:22).

Assignment

4 Draw a map of pre-1800 buildings in your city, town or village. Write notes on the location and use of these buildings over the years.

THE RURAL LANDSCAPE

Change was also affecting the countryside in the post-medieval period. The enclosure of fields for pasture was associated with a reduction in the number of hamlets and villages in England.

In the eighteenth century reorganization of the rural landscape also involved the creation of regularly shaped arable fields centred upon large country houses. Thus a fragmented pattern of irregularly shaped plots and fields was replaced by a landscape of larger fields and fewer settlements. Notable examples of eighteenth-

18

century mansions include Blenheim Palace, Bowood House and Harewood House. Of course large mansions in rural settings had been a long standing feature of the pattern of settlement. Examples of sixteenth-century mansions include Chatsworth (rebuilt 1687-1707), Longleat and Sherborne. Many landowners built new villages on their estates. The planned village movement was especially prominent in the north-east of Scotland with settlements such as Macduff and Gordonstown but the fashion was widely adopted. Other examples include Ormiston in East Lothian, Eaglesham to the south of Glasgow, Crieff and Callander. Some were purely intended as farm villages but others had other purposes such as fishing villages or small industrial centres. In time some of these planned villages developed into service centres of considerable local importance, e.g. Crieff and Callander. Many country houses acquired landscaped gardens in the eighteenth century mainly as a result of the designs created by Capability Brown (1716-83). Large mansions in landscaped gardens (Fig. 1:23) along with planned villages remain as distinctive relics of new settlement forms dating from the eighteenth century.

In the nineteenth century the number of farms increased and large farms became very distinctive landscape elements with various specialized buildings such as stables, byres, barns and rows of cottages to house the farm labourers. These large farms, especially in arable areas, were almost small hamlets. The fashion for the erection of country houses also continued, but many of the new houses were owned by wealthy merchants and industrialists whereas the earlier examples had been predominantly the property of the land-owning nobility.

Fig. 1:23
Bowood House, Wiltshire. Home of the Earl and Countess of Shelburne. The substantial mansion stands in a planned rural landscape of parkland, gardens and a lake.

Industrialization and Urban Growth

The upheaval in economic and social life named the Industrial Revolution encouraged a major phase of urban growth in Britain. Similar growth occurred slightly later in other Western European countries and in the north-eastern region of the United States of America.

At different periods in history the importance of a specific function has resulted in the concentration of people into towns and cities. In earlier times defence was vital but in the nineteenth century towns and cities flourished because of their rôles as centres of industry and trade. Some towns concentrated upon a particular industry such as the cotton-mill towns of Lancashire or the colliery towns of Durham. Other settlements became important **transport nodes** such as Crewe and Swindon, two important railway engineering centres. Seaside resorts developed to satisfy the recreational requirements of day-trippers from the major industrial regions. The market towns and administrative centres of the medieval period remained alongside the new and enlarged industrial towns and cities for the evolution of the settlement pattern through time is like a series of overlays each dating from a particular period. Previous patterns persist. Individual settlements may grow or decline depending upon their ability to adapt to the new factors encouraging growth. At the regional scale some areas become more important with new settlements mushrooming in response to the factors encouraging growth. We will return to the topic of the functions of settlements in Chapter 2.

In 1750 about 11 million people lived in Britain. By 1911 the population was 45 million. In 1750 about two in every three workers were engaged in agriculture whereas in 1911 it was less than one in ten. The changes in the distribution of population in the first half of the nineteenth century are shown in Figs. 1:24 and 1:25. From 1750 the percentage of the total population living in urban centres increased but the total number of people living in rural areas did not decrease until after 1851. Of course, some rural areas were losing more people to the cities than the rate of population increase long before 1851 but for Britain as a whole rural population reached its maximum in the 1851 Census.

Assignment

5 Select an industrial town or city and compare maps of the town at the beginning and end of the nineteenth century. Make a list of the main changes.

Causes of Urban Growth

People moved to the industrial towns and cities because of the attraction of employment opportunities and the push provided by declining job prospects in many rural areas. At first, industrialization did not necessarily involve factories or demand the concentration of the workforce in towns and cities but more complex machinery and higher output soon led to that situation. Closely-spaced industrial villages and towns grew in the nineteenth century to create conurbations (Fig. 1:26) such as Clydeside, Tyneside or the West Midlands (the Black Country). Each conurbation had a particular cluster of specializations related to local supplies or materials and the history of industrial development in that area, but engineering and the manufacturing of finished goods, be it cloth or ships, provided the economic base of each conurbation. All the people attracted to the mushrooming urban areas required services such as housing, food and medical care and specialized facilities developed to satisfy these needs. In turn, this meant that many people were employed in these service activities. This was also a period of growth for shops, banks, offices, hospitals and a wide array of specialized services.

Interdependent production processes such as the manufacture of parts or of semi-finished goods encouraged the process of concentration and subsequent industrial growth in established manufacturing centres. Of course, some pioneer developments proved to be badly located when the major phase of development occurred. Many

Fig. 1:24 Distribution of population in Britain early in the 19th century (R. LAWTON).

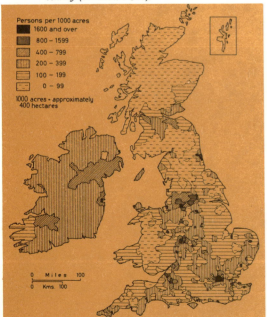

Fig. 1:25 Distribution of population in Britain at the middle of the 19th century (R. LAWTON).

remained in operation for several decades as minor pockets of industrialization in predominantly rural areas, the brick chimneys striking a strange chord in the composition of the landscape but others disappeared as competition soon eliminated the less profitable locations.

Urban Improvements

The rapid growth of towns and cities in the nineteenth century produced problems of inadequate housing, high population densities and unhealthy living environments. Various attempts were made by public-spirited individuals and groups to sponsor better housing for workers and local authorities gradually introduced regulations about housing conditions. Some writers speculated about completely different settlements. Of these the most effective was Ebenezer Howard. His writings on Garden Cities led to the building of the New Towns of Letchworth and Welwyn

Fig. 1:26 British conurbations.

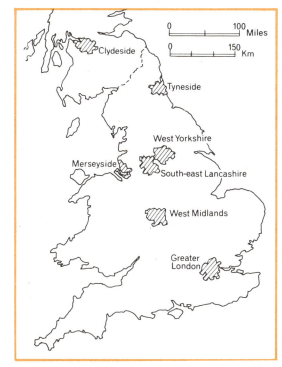

Garden City near London early in the present century. These towns were seen as offering a solution to the problems of the industrial cities by creating independent towns of about 50000

people with low population densities and attractively planned environments (Fig. 1:27). In effect, they would reverse the trend towards the concentration of people and buildings in major cities and direct migration toward planned urban environments.

Fig. 1:27 A housing area in Welwyn Garden City. The large number of trees and the spacious design of houses and roads illustrate the garden city ideal.

Dispersion and Decentralization

These two processes involved the movement of people to the edge of the city from the centre (decentralization) and to the rural-urban fringe and other settlements (dispersion). Both processes were well established by the end of the nineteenth century with the growth of low density suburbs and commuter settlements as people sought open space and healthy environments in which to raise a family. The trend towards outward, or centrifugal, movement was assisted by transport improvements such as suburban railways or tramways.

Until 1945 movement to the suburbs (decentralization) was dominant but subsequently the creation of New Towns (Fig. 1:28), expanded towns and new communities (e.g. Erskine near Glasgow and Cramlington near Newcastle) introduced major growth of planned settlements (dispersion).

In Fig. 1:29, the changing distribution of population in Greater London illustrates the nineteenth-century period of concentration of population into the city, followed by the more recent periods of decentralization and dispersion. The population of Inner London reached a peak in 1901. Suburban growth and then the development of New Towns channelled growth between 1900 and 1960 into the outer ring of Greater London. More recently, the decline of population in the outer ring reflects migration to more distant commuting areas beyond the fringing uplands of the Chilterns and Downs and the increased importance of expanded towns such as Swindon and the most recent New Towns such as Peterborough, Northampton and Milton Keynes. Peterborough and Northampton were both established towns but the site of Milton Keynes embraced several smaller settlements set within a predominantly rural landscape.

Within urban settlements the inner areas have been redeveloped and high population densities have been lowered by moving people to peripheral housing developments and to New Towns. These points will be developed in Chapters 4 and 5.

Rural Change

In rural areas changes are still taking place. In many regions people are still leaving the countryside and migrating to towns and cities. The loss of population creates an imbalance in the age structure of many rural communities and affects the viability of the provision of services such as primary schools in these areas.

In places out-migration is partly offset by the increase in the number of second homes and the houses of retired people. These points are developed in Chapter 6.

Commuting

The term refers to the situation where place of work and place of residence are in different communities, requiring daily journey, or travel, to work. Transport developments have extended the potential commuting distance (Fig. 1:30). Express trains and motorways mean that major cities can have a commuting hinterland with a radius in excess of one hundred kilometres. However, decentralization and dispersion have now affected the location of industry and offices. Many of these 'land uses' have now moved out of the large cities into the suburban fringe or to New Towns and expanded towns on the outer edge of the commuting hinterland of the major cities. This has produced a more dispersed and complex settlement pattern with workplace-residence linkages between many different nodes or settlements. This situation exists around metropolitan centres such as London or Paris or Tokyo or New York or Sydney. Indeed it is found

Fig. 1:28 British New Towns.

Fig. 1:29 Population zones of Greater London 1801-1977.

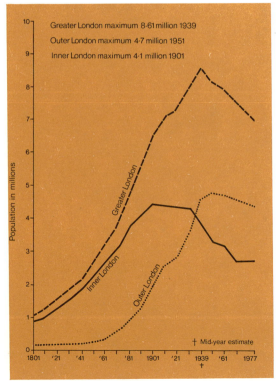

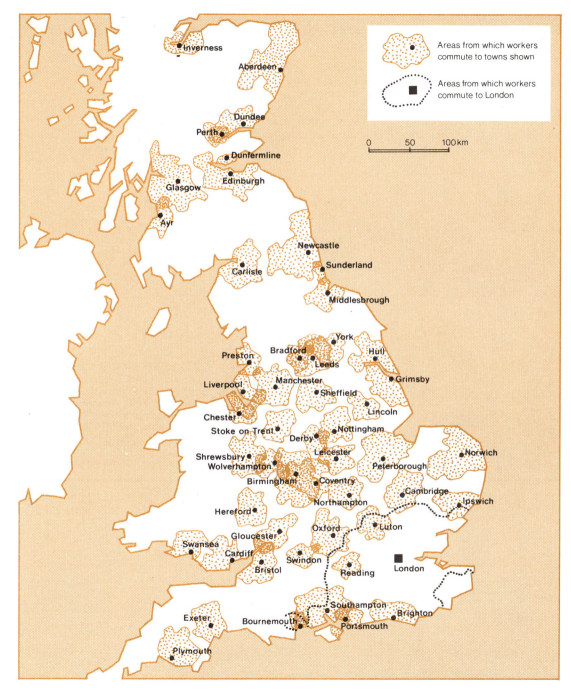

wherever decentralization and dispersion have occurred in highly urbanized situations in economically developed countries.

By contrast, in developing countries the principal processes are those associated with the attraction of people to cities, the concentration of population and economic activity in the limited space of the urban area of the city. Reference will be made in Chapter 5 to features of the rapid urbanization in developing countries including the growth of squatter settlements within and on the edge of many cities.

Fig. 1:30 Commuting zones of British towns and cities. A small number of people commute very large distances but the majority live within one hours' journey time of the town or city. In the most populated regions people can live within one hours' travelling time of several settlements. This can increase the economic opportunities open to the individual and give a large potential labour force for new industries and a large market for new shops and services.

Areas from which workers commute to towns shown

Areas from which workers commute to London

0   50   100 km

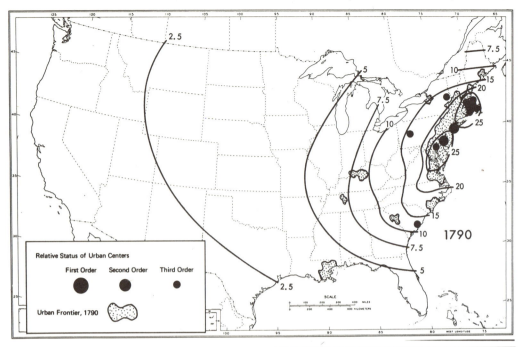

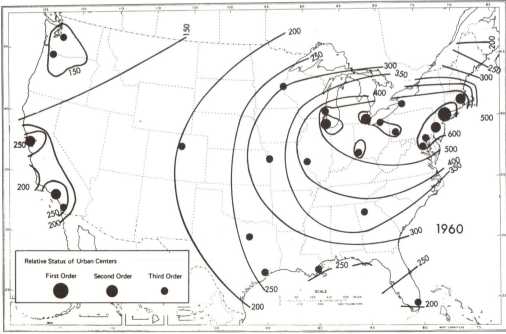

Fig. 1:31 *American urban centres in 1790. The contours show population potential in relation to the largest cities. The wide spacing of the lines west of the Appalachians reflects the sparseness of the population in that region.*

Fig. 1:32 *Population potentials, USA, 1960. Compared to Fig. 1:31 there has been a great increase in the number of cities and a westward movement of population. There are major cities in the West e.g. Los Angeles, San Francisco and Seattle, the Mid-West (Chicago) and the South (New Orleans, Houston, Dallas). (BERRY and HORTON.)*

Settlement Evolution in the New World

In the New World countries of North America and Australasia settlement evolution has largely been confined to the last few centuries. The comparative newness of the pattern removes some of the complexity found in Western Europe. Nonetheless, change can occur in a few decades so that the pattern in the U.S.A. has evolved and changed in the few centuries since the voyage of discovery by Columbus. Figs. 1:31 and 1:32 illustrate the evolution of the pattern between 1790 and 1960. The maps show a westward movement in the centre of population distribution and the development of cities in the Mid-West, South and West. The westward movement of pioneers involved the creation of numerous farms and homesteads, villages and towns, in addition to a small number of major urban centres which became the cities of these regions. This process of peopling the American landscape was broadly equivalent to the founding of farms, villages and boroughs in England in the period between the Domesday Book survey and the sixteenth century.

The decision of the American government to adopt a grid base for surveying the lands west of the Appalachians has profoundly influenced the spacing and form of farms, villages and towns in this vast region (Fig. 1:33).

Other Factors Affecting Settlement Evolution

Elsewhere in the world some settlements have ancient origins and have evolved in response to the culture and history of that particular society. Thus, in areas once under colonial rule, the imperial powers influenced the pattern of settlement to achieve trading and administrative goals.

In general the structure of a settlement is influenced by the values of the society. In Britain or North America the prime sites in the city centre tend to be occupied by major stores, whereas in Islamic societies the mosque occupies a primary location in the settlement. We can describe basic types of cities which represent major cultural differences such as those between European and American cities, Islamic cities, Asian cities and Socialist (Russian) cities and these will be discussed in Chapter 4.

Assignment

6 Compare Figs. 1:34, 1:35, 1:36, and 1:37. Make a list of the main features shown in each photograph. Make a list of the main differences between each pair of photographs. To what extent could these differences be due to cultural differences?

Conclusion

Sometimes very different aspects of settlement evolution occur at the same time. The pioneer phase of the wagon train in America was coincident with the emergence of major cities such as New York on the eastern seaboard. The cowboy and the settler were greatly outnumbered by the number of Americans living in established villages, towns and cities east of the Mississippi.

Different trends can occur in different parts of the world. Thus people are being attracted to cities in developing countries at the same time as the processes of outward movement, dispersion and decentralization, dominate the situation in developed countries.

Rapid population growth in developing countries may mean that the maximum rural population has still to be reached, although the proportion of

Fig. 1:33 An example of the grid-iron division of land, Salt Lake City.

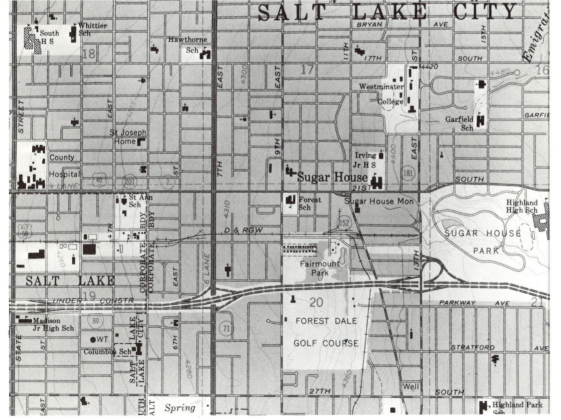

the population living in towns and cities is rapidly increasing.

You should be careful to avoid over-simplified views of settlement geography. The flood of migrants to the cities in developing countries is a good example of this situation. Housing problems obviously exist in these countries but we should not imagine that all inhabitants of these cities live in slums. Nor is housing the only type of land use in these cities. There are office blocks and modern shops, numerous workshops and open-air markets. The pattern of land use is complex and varied in terms of quality of property, types of materials and location of uses, just as we would expect it to be in a British or American city. The differences in appearance of the buildings and the differences in the location of the uses are important but you should not think of Calcutta or any other city in a developing country as some sort of elementary city but rather one reflecting particular cultural, historical and economic conditions.

Finally, change will continue to occur. Some places will become more important, others stagnate or even decline. In Britain since 1945 New Towns have increased in importance whereas major cities have decreased in population size. What do you think will happen to the settlement pattern in Britain between now and the year 2000 AD? Will suburban growth stop? Will the New Towns stabilize at their present population size? Will rural areas continue to lose population by migration to urban areas?

Planning can seek to favour some trends and oppose other developments. Other important factors include the state of the economy, improvements in communications, and changes in taste such as housing fashions.

Fig. 1:35 Singapore.

Fig. 1:36 Nkongsamba, Cameroon.

Assignment

7 Write a brief essay explaining the major changes which you think will occur in the settlement pattern of Great Britain, and especially in your local area, up to the year 2000 AD.

Revision Questions

1 How would you define a settlement?

2 Explain why it is often difficult to distinguish between settlements of different sizes. How does the term town vary from country to country, region to region?

3 What do you understand by the following terms: urbanization; conurbation; megalopolis; metropolis?
Give examples of the last three in terms of the countries in which they are found and the city areas involved.

4 Describe the main differences between: Pre-Roman, Roman and medieval settlements in Britain.

5 Explain how the Industrial Revolution affected
(a) Rural settlement in Britain
(b) The growth of cities in Britain

6 List the main factors involved in urban growth in Britain from the late eighteenth century.

7 What do the terms dispersion and decentralization mean when applied to urban areas?

Fig. 1:37 Tbilisi, USSR.

CHAPTER TWO

CLASSIFICATION OF SETTLEMENT

By grouping settlements into types we can highlight similarities, since members of a group should possess common features relating to the criteria used to produce the groups. Commonly used criteria include: **Function, Size, Site** and **Situation**. Settlements will have characteristics relating to each criterion but membership of a common set based on one factor, e.g. function, may not necessarily correlate with the groupings based on another factor such as size (see Fig. 2:1). Equally, linkages can occur between different aspects, e.g. site may influence function. We classify settlements in an attempt to reduce the vast array of potential information to a meaningful organized structure. The test of success is the extent to which members of a class are similar and distinct from members of other classes.

A major method of settlement classification is that based upon function. There are two main variants: those based upon dominant function and those which involve a broader assessment of the mix of functions in settlements. Certain functions are found in almost every settlement but others only occur in certain places. Fig. 2:2 lists various functions performed by settlements.

Assignment
1 Separate the functions listed in Fig. 2:2 into two groups:
   (a) Ubiquitous (found in almost every settlement)
   (b) Specialized (found only in certain settlements).

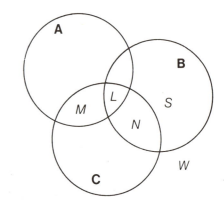

A is the set of large settlements (cities) — over 400 000 people (settlements classified according to size)

B is the set of settlements on strategic sites — bridging points or fording points on rivers (settlements classified according to site)

C is the set of settlements which are manufacturing towns or cities (settlements classified according to function)

Settlement *L* (London) belongs to all three groups — a large manufacturing town/city on a strategic site

Settlement *M* (Manchester) is a large manufacturing town/city

Settlement *N* (Sunderland) is a manufacturing town on a strategic site

Settlement *S* (Stirling) is a small town on a strategic site

Settlement *W* (Worthing) is a resort, not on a bridging point or fording point, without important manufacturers.

Fig. 2:1
Classification of settlements by sets.

We would probably all agree that the service and residential functions should appear in the first group and transport, market and port or gateway functions in the second group. Where you placed the others may depend upon the size of your own settlement. If you live in a city they probably appeared in the first group but if you live in a village many of the remaining functions may seem quite specialized. This illustrates some important points about classification. We need some measure of the general or average situation and of specific forms or levels of specialization.

Settlements are dynamic organisms. They are continually changing and this can alter the functional character. Some settlements which in the eighteenth century were primarily market towns became, in the nineteenth century, industrial towns. Now the major industry may be in decline and the administrative or local government function may be the most important function of the settlement.

A further point is that we expect the classes to assist our study of settlements. Membership of a functional group should paint a picture about the employment structure, the economy, the type of land use and even the physical appearance of the landscape of the settlement. Thus it may be necessary to recognize sub-categories of particular functional types. For example we can classify towns as being 'industrial' but we should recognize sub-groups such as 'mining', 'textiles', 'iron and steel' or 'electronics' because they do differ from each other in appearance, land use and economic structure.

How can we assess the Main Function of a Settlement?

The main problem here is to choose a reliable method which allows us to state with some degree of accuracy what is the chief function of a particular town. If we were simply to assume that the activity which employs the largest number of people was the main function of the town, we would find that in many cases towns would be classed as service centres since the service trades tend to employ the largest number of people in most settlements. This problem can be overcome by using data relating to the percentage of people employed in different activities to define a particular level of specialization. One study carried out in the United States in the 1940s identified the following eight functional types of settlements: **1.** Manufacturing **2.** Retail **3.** Wholesale **4.** Diversified **5.** Transportation **6.** Mining **7.** University **8.** Resort or Retirement (Fig. 2:3).

Each category was represented by a minimum percentage of employed people in specific occupations. Thus to be classed as a wholesale centre, there had to be at least 20 per cent of the total employed population engaged in wholesaling and this had to equal at least 45 per cent of the number employed in retailing. This study did recognize

Retail-Wholesale and Service Functions
This function refers to the different kinds of shops, wholesale premises and service facilities offered by a settlement. This function is referred to as the Central Place function. There are many sub-groups of retail and service establishments and the presence or absence of particular groups may be closely linked to the population size of settlements.

Industrial Functions
This refers to the various types of industrial premises found within the boundaries of a settlement. It relates chiefly to primary (extractive) and secondary (manufacturing) groups of economic activity since the tertiary (offices and shops) group is already accounted for above.

Administrative Functions
These functions are concerned with the various types of local and central government establishments offered by a settlement. These range from local council offices to central and regional government offices.

Educational Functions
Depending upon the level of economic and social development of individual countries, settlements may have various forms of educational institutions. These range from primary schools to universities and colleges of further education.

Residential Functions
This refers to the various buildings which meet the accommodation needs of the settlement's inhabitants. Depending upon the size of the settlement a wide variety of buildings may be identified ranging from high density, low cost housing to high cost detached houses in private estates. In third world countries, an extra dimension may be added viz, that of 'Shanty town dwellings', which are often found on the outskirts of large towns and cities.

Recreational and Entertainment Functions
These include cinemas, theatres, sport centres, clubs, public parks and golf courses. Again the number and variety present may reflect the site of the settlement.

Transport Functions
These refer to the various forms of transport facilities provided and include centres which are particularly important in terms of road, rail, water or air transport.

Market Functions
This refers to settlements which offer an agricultural market place for the sale of livestock and farm produce. Traders may visit the settlement only on special days of the week or month, the market days.

Port or Gateway Functions
These are special facilities geared to importing and exporting goods. In the case of ports, the goods are normally transported by water but gateways can be located inland. Cities such as Calgary form a gateway function for the Prairie Provinces of Canada. Here goods can be carried by various forms of transport including rail, road, air or pipeline. Nonetheless, special facilities exist to store and distribute goods and to ensure a speedy transfer of imports and exports for the region.

Fig. 2:2 Settlement Functions

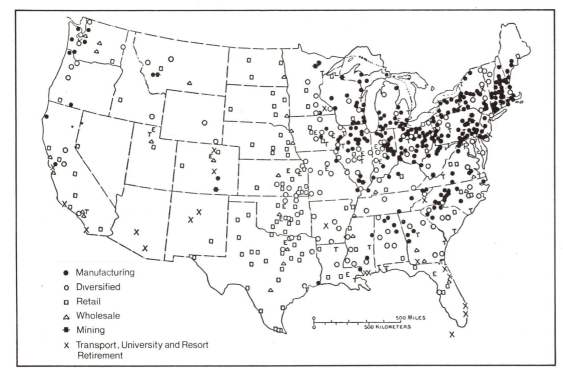

Legend:
- ● Manufacturing
- ○ Diversified
- □ Retail
- △ Wholesale
- ✚ Mining
- ✕ Transport, University and Resort Retirement

500 MILES
500 KILOMETERS

Fig. 2:3 A functional classification of American cities (C. D. HARRIS). Some types of settlements, such as manufacturing centres, are located in relation to materials, energy sources or markets. By contrast retail centres are more widespread and reflect the distribution of population.

Fig. 2:4 Order of centres in Southern Germany in 1930 (W. CHRISTALLER).

Rank or Order		Type of centre	Number of Places	Population
L	Landstadt	(Regional Capital City)	1	500 000
P	Provinzstadt	(Provincial Head City)	2	100 000
G	Gaustadt	(Small State Capital)	6	30 000
B	Bezirkstadt	(District City)	18	10 000
K	Kreissstadt	(County Seat)	54	4000
A	Amstort	(Township Centre)	162	2000
M	Markort	(Market Town)	486	1000

that the eight functional types were not comprehensive and that other specialist centres could exist such as State capitals or fishing settlements.

Another study was able to classify 897 towns and cities in America on the basis of ten major functional categories: **1.** Manufacturing **2.** Retail **3.** Professional Services **4.** Transport and Communication **5.** Personal Services **6.** Public Administration **7.** Wholesale **8.** Mining **9.** Financial Services and Real Estate **10.** Diversified. This study showed that about 27 per cent of the settlements were diversified (they had no particular specialization but included a wide variety of functions) and a further 20 per cent had some specialization in manufacturing. In contrast to these major classes, some functional specialisms were less common. For example, about 11 per cent of all settlements had an above average degree of employment in transportation while less than 10 per cent of settlements had a degree of specialization in public administration. In this classification settlements can show above average levels of employment in more than one function so that it was possible to identify some associations between specialisms in particular settlements. It does, therefore, illustrate the second variant mentioned earlier, classification based on the mixture of functional specialization. In general both classifications show that some functional types are more commonly found than others.

Since all settlements perform a service function to some degree, it is appropriate to begin our discussion of dominant functional types by looking at Service Centres.

Towns as Service Centres

The study of service centres has attracted a great deal of attention from geographers for many years. Their attempts to classify or group settlements has led to the emergence of a body of theory governing the function, distribution and relationship between centres and their surrounding regions, known as **Central Place Theory**. Basically, this theory suggests that service centres can be grouped into a distinct series of orders. Each succeeding order or level contains settlements which are more important than the order below in the hierarchy. The importance of a settlement is measured in terms of factors such as the variety and number of retail and service facilities offered within the settlement. These facilities are called **Central Place functions**. In effect, the settlements are grouped into what is described as a **Central Place hierarchy**. The ideas concerning this arrangement of service centres were first postulated by the German geographer Walter Christaller. Working in Southern Germany, he produced the following hierarchy of centres (Fig. 2:4).

Christaller based his assessment of functional status on measurements derived from data relating to the number of telephones present within the settlements in his study area. Since that time, however, the use of the telephone has changed. It is no longer a useful measure of the commercial importance of a centre since it is now used by a large number of domestic users. Most studies which followed Christaller referred to other service functions. Fig. 2:5 illustrates the types of functions used in a study of service centres in Snohomish County, in the Mid-West of the U.S.A. You will notice that the functional types listed are establishments basically concerned with the provision of goods and services to people living within the study area. In other words certain settlement functions are ignored, such as industrial and residential functions.

The principal characteristics of Christaller's hierarchy involve four relationships. First, the centres are grouped into distinct levels, ranging from low to high order centres. Terms such as 1st order, 2nd order and so on are often used to describe the various layers of the hierarchy. Other terms such as hamlet, village, town and city are also frequently used to describe orders of the hierarchy although these terms can vary in exact meaning in different countries and at different periods in history.

Secondly, many studies have shown that a definite relationship exists between the functional importance (which could be measured by the types of shops and services offered) and the population sizes of the settlements. This relationship is shown in Fig. 2:6. Some geographers argue that this gives us some idea of what to expect in terms of the functional status of settlements of different population sizes. However it is not always as simple as that statement might imply. Many factors can complicate the situation. For example, it has

Fig. 2:5 List of functions used in an American study of service centres.

Number of Activities

Petrol Stations
Food Stores
Churches
Restaurants
Public Houses
Elementary Schools
Doctors
Estate Agents
Electrical Appliance Stores
Hairdressers
Car Dealers
Insurance Agents
Bulk Oil Distributors
Dentists
Motels
Hardware Stores
Car Repair Works
Fuel Dealers (coal; etc.)
Drug Stores
Beauticians
Motor Spares Dealers
Meeting Halls
Animal Feed Stores
Lawyers
Furniture Stores, etc.
Variety Stores
Road Haulage Firms & Warehouses
Veterinaries
Clothing Stores
Timber Yards & Woodworking
Banks
Farm Implement Dealers
Electrical Repair Shops
Florists
High Schools
Dry Cleaners
Local Taxi Services
Billiard Hall & Bowling Alleys
Jewellery Stores
Hotels
Cobblers
Sporting Goods Stores
Frozen Foods Stores
Department Stores
Opticians
Hospital and Clinics
Undertakers
Photographers
Chartered Accountants
Laundries and Laundromats
Health Practitioners

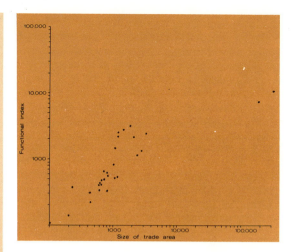

Fig. 2:6 There is a relationship between the service importance of a place and the number of people living in that place.

been shown that towns which specialize in industrial functions often do not have the array of shops and services which might be expected for their population size. This is explained by the fact that these towns do not attract the 'normal' level of trade from people living in the surrounding area. In other words the service hinterland of such settlements is smaller than we might expect on the basis of the population resident in the Central Place. This point is explained in greater detail in Chapter 3.

Thirdly, the hierarchy of centres, based on the number and type of service establishments present, implies that there is also a hierarchy of goods and services, i.e. functions. In effect, certain good such as furniture are of a higher order than other goods such as groceries or newspapers. We purchase the lower order goods more frequently than the higher order goods. One consequence is that we need a large number of centres supplying low order goods and a much smaller number of centres specializing in higher order goods, because we are willing to travel further, and spend more time and money, in our search for a suitable good of a higher order such as a suite of furniture. The relative importance of Central Place functions has been illustrated in many studies and, indeed, in some instances the determination of settlement hierarchies has been based on the assumption that particular establishments are indicative of a distinct level in the hierarchy. A. E. Smailes, in a study in the 1940s of towns and cities in England and Wales, referred to certain establishments such as named banks and stores, cinemas, the publication of a local newspaper and specialized services such as a hospital and a secondary school as basic indicators of different levels of the hierarchy. Settlements had to possess this basic cluster of establishments in order to qualify for the functional status of town in the Smailes hierarchy. He produced the settlement hierarchy shown in Fig. 2:7. Since

then there have been arguments about the validity of using particular establishments as indicators of hierarchical ordering which has led to various refinements in the methods used to determine the centrality value of service centres. Some of these are discussed in Chapter 7.

The fourth point is that centres in each succeeding level of the hierarchy should possess the ability to supply the goods and services found within centres at lower levels. Again research in a variety of geographical settings has shown that this is essentially true. This concept, which is termed **nesting of Central Place functions**, is illustrated by Fig. 2:8.

As we mentioned earlier, Central Place Theory is not only concerned with the classification of settlements into a hierarchical ordering based on functional status. It is also concerned with the relationships between centres and the areas which they serve. Furthermore, it deals with the impact which this particular relationship has on the spatial distribution of settlements and on the shape of their trade areas. Chapter 3 will examine these

horizontal (spacing of centres and shape of trade areas) and vertical (hierarchy of centres and functions) components of Central Places in greater detail.

One final point which we should consider is whether there is an alternative arrangement of centres to that of the hierarchy proposed earlier. Some writers have suggested that there is an alternative structure. G. K. Zipf, for instance, suggested that instead of a series of distinct grades of settlements, a more likely arrangement would be that in which the population size of settlements formed a smooth curve when plotted on a graph, as shown in Fig. 2:9. This is called the **Rank-Size Rule**. Zipf claimed that the second largest city in a country would be half of the population size of the largest. The third largest would have one third the population of the first, the fourth — one quarter, and so on. Cities in the U.S.A. and in other parts of the world have been shown to broadly conform to this pattern although particular settlements were sometimes larger or smaller than expected for their rank in the order

Fig. 2:7 Urban hierarchy of England and Wales in 1940s (A. E. SMAILES). Subsequent changes include the growth of New Towns and suburban centres and decline of some industrial and mining settlements.

Fig. 2:8 Nesting of central place functions in Ayrshire.

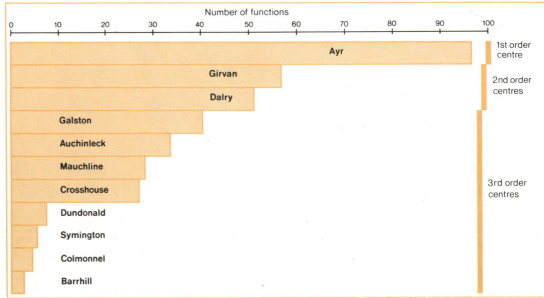

of settlements. In other cases, the second largest city has often been shown to have only a third to a quarter of the population of the first. Where that situation occurs, the largest city is known as a Primate City because it is much larger than the other major settlements in the country and exercises primacy in the settlement system. London is an example of this situation.

Many geographers have argued that far from contradicting the notion of a hierarchy, the ideas contained in the Rank Size Rule may, in fact, be quite compatible with them. They point out that the Zipf rule is based solely on population size whereas hierarchies are based on measurement of functional complexity. It is possible that both systems co-exist. If functional complexity was regarded as including all urban functions, rather than only service functions, the pattern might be transformed from a hierarchy to a more continuous arrangement when measured by the population size of the settlements.

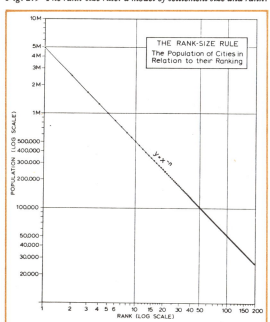

Fig. 2:9 *The rank-size rule: a model of settlement size and rank.*

We will return to a consideration of the methods used to assess the functional status of Central Place functions and Central Places in Chapter 7.

Other Major Functional Types

As you will have gathered, classifications based on the service functions of settlements do not account for all functional types. We shall examine seven other types: (**a**) Industrial towns (**b**) Market towns (**c**) Resorts (**d**) University towns (**e**) Religious centres (**f**) Political and regional capitals (**g**) Ports.

INDUSTRIAL CENTRES

This functional specialization can occur in various types of settlements from towns to vast urban complexes. Fig. 2:10 shows the pattern of employment in the West Midlands Economic Planning Region, a large part of Central England which includes the specialized industrial centres of Birmingham, Coventry (vehicles), Wolverhampton (metal works and engineering) and Stoke (potteries). The area also includes a considerable amount of farmland and numerous commuter villages and market towns. We normally divide employment into three broad

sectors, viz. primary (extractive); secondary (manufacturing); tertiary (offices and shops). Although the West Midlands is an important manufacturing region, employment in that sector provides only 49.7 per cent of all jobs in that area. In general over the last fifty years, the percentage of British population employed in tertiary occupations has steadily increased whilst that in manufacturing has continually declined.

We can see the marked concentration of particular industries in specific English conurbations in 1931 in Fig. 2:11. Notice the importance of metal trades in Birmingham and textiles in Manchester and the West Riding. Tyneside presents a complex picture but shipbuilding and marine activities are both shown in the employment figures for metal trades and fishing. Some activities occur at a fairly constant level in all of the conurbations, e.g. construction and commerce.

Assignment

2 Compare the data shown in Figs. 2:10 and 2:11 and describe the changes in the tertiary employment sector between 1931 and 1976. Can you account for these changes?

Fig. 2:10 *Employment, 1976, in West Midlands (in thousands).*

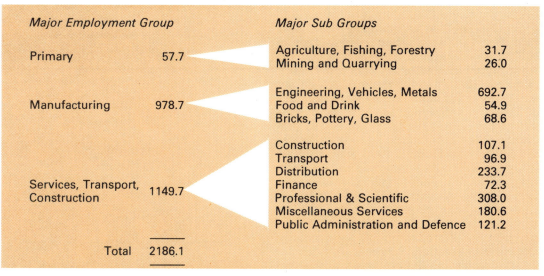

Major Employment Group		Major Sub Groups	
Primary	57.7	Agriculture, Fishing, Forestry	31.7
		Mining and Quarrying	26.0
Manufacturing	978.7	Engineering, Vehicles, Metals	692.7
		Food and Drink	54.9
		Bricks, Pottery, Glass	68.6
Services, Transport, Construction	1149.7	Construction	107.1
		Transport	96.9
		Distribution	233.7
		Finance	72.3
		Professional & Scientific	308.0
		Miscellaneous Services	180.6
		Public Administration and Defence	121.2
Total	2186.1		

Fig. 2:11 Employment in the English conurbations, 1931.

KEY (Fig. 2:11):
- 1 Commerce
- 2 Personal service & entertainment
- 3 Agriculture, fishing, mining
- 4 Metal trades
- 5 Textiles
- 6 Leather, clothing
- 7 Wood, paper
- 8 Food, drink
- 9 Chemicals
- 10 Brick, pottery, glass
- 11 Administration
- 12 Transport
- 13 Construction
- 14 Professional services
- 15 Miscellaneous

BIRMINGHAM / MANCHESTER / TYNESIDE / WEST RIDING (Leeds/Bradford)

Industry can be attracted to particular locations because of factors such as the availability of raw materials, markets, transport and labour plus the intervention of government in the form of grants and subsidies. Local resources may encourage the development of an industrial region but this can also occur because a particular area acquires a reputation for a particular activity, e.g. Sheffield — cutlery, Birmingham — guns and jewellery, Leeds — woollen products.

During the nineteenth century, distinctive townscapes developed in various industrial regions such as the textile mills and brick-terraced houses of Lancashire (cotton), Yorkshire (wool), the bottle-shaped kilns of the Potteries and the blast furnaces of the iron and steel towns such as Consett, Corby and Middlesbrough and the shipyards of Tyneside, Merseyside and Clydeside. Some settlements became the centres of British production of particular goods, e.g. jute in Dundee and linoleum in Kirkcaldy and Staines. Other industries were very widespread and found in many towns, e.g. iron foundries, breweries or confectionery. Another trend in the twentieth century has been the gradual closure of many small factories and mills in small towns and the concentration of production in a few very large plants in major centres. One result of this trend is that many towns which were classed as industrial

centres several decades ago can no longer claim this title since they now lack a major manufacturing element in their employment structure.

Fig. 2:12 Principal male occupations, Motherwell and Wishaw, 1971.

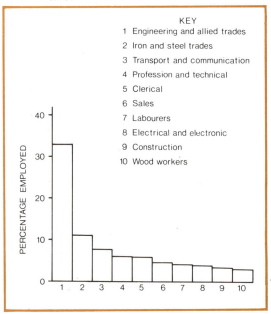

KEY
1 Engineering and allied trades
2 Iron and steel trades
3 Transport and communication
4 Profession and technical
5 Clerical
6 Sales
7 Labourers
8 Electrical and electronic
9 Construction
10 Wood workers

Case Study 1—Motherwell, Lanarkshire

A fine example of an industrial town in Britain is that of Motherwell in Lanarkshire in Central Scotland. Fig. 2:12 shows the employment structure of this town. Notice the predominance of manufacturing industry in the town. A major employer is the British Steel Corporation's steelworks at Ravenscraig, which was opened in 1958. This new integrated plant provided much needed employment for Motherwell and the surrounding areas. Some local industries were in serious decline, e.g. coal mines and textiles. Iron and steel-making and engineering have been the mainstays of employment since the late nineteenth century. Recently several new industries have been established in the town in an effort to diversify the industrial structure. These included light engineering and electrical goods. Nevertheless the town retains its character as a major centre of heavy industry and the large integrated strip mill at Ravenscraig still dominates the landscape. Despite the difficulties experienced in the iron and steel industry in recent years, Ravenscraig has maintained its importance as one of the leading plants in Britain although economic recession and plant closure in other allied industries in the area, e.g. car manufacturing (Linwood) and shipbuilding (Upper Clyde) make its future less secure.

Assignment

3 Compare the industrial townscapes in Figs. 2:13 and 2:14 and suggest which townscape is typical of the twentieth century. List the main features of each example, e.g. type of industry, style of buildings, etc.

Fig. 2:13 *A 19th century industrial landscape. This view of Blackburn shows the importance of canals as a means of transporting coal in the early stages of the growth of the textile industry. Notice the close association between the streets of terraced houses and the factories.*

Fig. 2:14 *Modern industrial landscape of Stevenage New Town. Note the low factory-buildings which are set apart. The factories are close to major roads, the principal form of transport being by lorry. There are no houses on the photograph but there are areas of green space.*

MINING CENTRES

In mining centres extractive industry is the dominant function. Some mining towns have more than 30000 residents but they are more commonly in the 2000-10000 size category. Mining centres often lack the number and variety of shops and services which might be expected for service centres of the same population size because they do not serve a surrounding agricultural hinterland. In Britain, the cooperative store dominates the retail provision. Elsewhere company stores are often the chief source of goods and supplies.

Case Study 2—Weipa: North Queensland, Australia

With a population of about 2300, the North Queensland (Australia) town of Weipa is a major supplier of bauxite. The people living in Weipa are provided with various commercial and entertainment facilities including a cinema, a supermarket, several shops, a school, a medical centre, a police station and a bank. The residential areas consist primarily of single-storey apartments located on the northern and southern margins of the peninsula (Fig. 2:15). Swamps have prevented housing developments in other directions. Apart from the mining activities, the industries include a refinery which was opened in 1973. The port at Lorim point, which handles bauxite exports to Japan and Europe, is connected to the mining areas by a railway. In addition, a small airstrip gives the possibility of rapid connections with major Australian cities for both business and services.

In remote situations such as Weipa, mining companies have to make special efforts to attract their workforce. These include offering high wages, good sports and recreational facilities, housing and schooling and communications with major urban areas. Nevertheless in very cold or hot countries it can be difficult to attract the necessary labour.

Mining centres can be ephemeral features of the landscape. This means that they are suddenly developed and often quickly abandoned in direct response to the demand and availability of particular mineral resources. Abandoned centres can become fossilized almost intact. On other occasions little remains of the settlement apart from spoil heaps left after the mine workings closed. In some cases mining centres became service centres and grew into important towns even though the mineral resource was exhausted or abandoned.

MARKET TOWNS

These settlements are usually located in rural areas and their chief function is to provide a market place for the sale of agricultural goods, produce, livestock and the provision of specialized services for the agricultural community. The settlement will also offer a fairly extensive range of other shops and services to the resident population and the population living within its general service area or hinterland. Ideally the market town should possess all of the features shown in the following diagram — Fig. 2:16.

Case Study 3—Malton (Fig. 2:17)

Situated almost equidistant from York and Scarborough on the junction of the A64 and the A619, Malton is the principal market town serving the rich agricultural region in the Vale of Pickering. The town functions both as a service centre and as an agricultural market centre. Livestock and agricultural produce is sold on Fridays and Saturdays, the town's market days. Adding to the nodality of the town is the fact that it is served by a bus and railway terminal. In fact, it is this market

Fig. 2:15 Weipa, an Australian mining settlement.

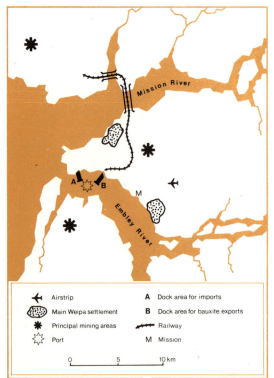

Airstrip	A Dock area for imports
Main Weipa settlement	B Dock area for bauxite exports
Principal mining areas	Railway
Port	M Mission

0   5   10 km

Fig. 2:16 Model of a market town.

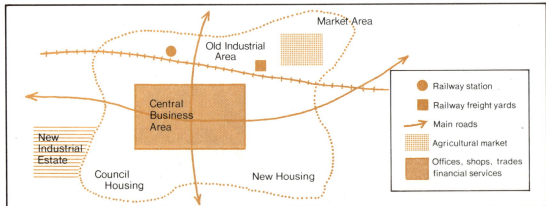

●	Railway station
■	Railway freight yards
→	Main roads
	Agricultural market
	Offices, shops, trades financial services

function which has allowed Malton to retain its identity. This is extremely important in this instance since Malton (pop. 4070), sited on the north bank of the Derwent, forms almost a 'twin-town' complex with Norton (pop. 5660) on the south bank of the river. The retention of its character and identity probably reflects the important influence which historical tradition has had on Malton's functional character.

In addition to its market function, Malton also provides a wide range of shops and other Central Place functions plus several industrial firms which offer an extensive range of employment opportunity. The amount and character of indus-trial activity in the town is illustrated in the following tables — Figs. 2:18 and 2:19.

Notice also the importance of agricultural employment for men and office and shop work for women.

We can compare Malton to the market town model in Fig. 2:16. The most obvious points of similarity are seen in terms of the agricultural market area, the range of shops, the provision of transport services and the general structural layout of both settlements. Major points of dissimilarity include the diverse range of industrial premises within Malton and the fact that Malton is situated in close proximity to another, larger settlement (Norton).

	Male	Female
Agriculture	14.3	4.3
Manufacturing	35.7	26.1
Construction	7.1	—
Public Utilities	2.4	—
Distribution	9.5	17.4
Miscellaneous Services	7.1	21.7
Public Administration	9.5	4.3
Professional Services & Transport	14.3	26.1

Fig. 2:18 Employment, Malton, 1976.

Fig. 2:19 Principal industries in Malton, 1980.

Agricultural Service Industries and Agricultural Suppliers

Pyramid Pids — manufacture and supply pig pens
Brandsby Agricultural Trading Association — supply feed and fertilizer etc.
Yorkshire and Northern Woolgrowers — supply feed and fertilizer etc.
Yates — agricultural equipment and machinery suppliers/services
2 Agricultural depots

General Services and Suppliers

Gabriel Wade — timber merchants
Sedmans — Lorry repairs
Ainsty Factoring — builders merchants
Crossleys — builders merchants
Park Engineering — engine repairs/rebuilders
Delmar — D.I.Y. product suppliers
Printers — 3

Manufacturers

Bright Steels — manufacture precision section steel rod, bar, etc.
Spectra-Tek — manufacture computer monitoring and control systems
Neaco — aluminium fabrications
Polliack — manufacture bathroom fittings
Pottery
Fertilizer Factory

Food Processors

Bowyers
Westlers

Fig. 2:17 The market town of Malton.

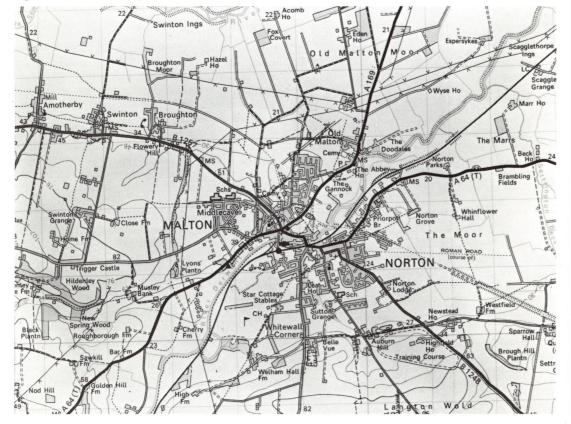

Case Study 4—Market Centres in South-West China (Fig. 2:20)

Studies, conducted some two decades ago, of market centres in South-West China revealed some interesting variations in terms of the form and distribution of market centres compared with those in Britain and Europe. For example, many small villages had no services at all. Only settlements in South-West China with populations in excess of 1000 persons offered market facilities. These differences primarily reflect cultural and economic circumstances in the respective countries. The provision of services is largely a reflection of the degree to which people require to buy goods and use services. Farmers with a considerable degree of self-sufficiency will have less need of market facilities than others producing specialized crops and animal products for sale in the market place. This feature is commonly associated with rural areas in Third World countries where the Central Place and market functions are simpler than those normally found in Europe or North America. One of the most noticeable characteristics of market centres in South-West China was the importance of 'periodic markets' in rural areas. Traders would visit the larger settlements regularly, perhaps once a week or once a month. These traders would offer a variety of manufactured goods such as clothes and hardware. More recently the pattern in South-West China has been altered by various decisions made by the government. Rural settlements now exist as 'production brigades', elements of the 'commune farming system' in Communist China. Equally the provision of services is now more formally structured with particular services located in various centres largely in relation to population distribution.

Despite the obvious differences between these case studies both areas display some similarities. The principal common characteristic is the function of market centres in rural communities. In both situations the centres provide a place for the sale, trading or collection of agricultural produce and livestock and the purchase or supply of goods, equipment and specialized services. In both cases certain basic facilities are required including access to the surrounding regions, by road and perhaps also by rail. An area must also be set aside in the market centres for a market place, the point of barter, exchange or sale of goods. It is these similarities which help us to identify towns within this particular functional category despite international differences in levels of economic development and methods of organization and administration.

RESORTS

Most of us have at one time or another visited a settlement at the coast during the summer months. The settlements which attract the greatest number of visitors during this time of the year usually offer a wide range of facilities specially designed to meet the needs of tourists. These would include a wide range of entertainments (theatres, cinemas, cafes, pubs, bingo halls and so on), and many different types of places where visitors can spend a few days including hotels, boarding houses and hostels. In effect, the settlement specializes in one particular function, viz. attracting a tourist trade. Most resorts will therefore try to use their particular sites to maximum advantage by, for example, providing a well maintained promenade behind a sandy beach. Most of the shops and businesses will reflect the needs of the tourists, e.g. toys and souvenirs, clothes shops, chemists and hairdressers. In many of the older resorts in Britain a pier is quite common, e.g. Blackpool, Bournemouth and Brighton. Sadly, many piers have fallen into disrepair because of lack of money to maintain them. Typical examples of seaside resorts are found throughout Britain and the coastal areas of Europe, particularly Brittany, western France and the Mediterranean and Adri-

Fig. 2:20 Market centres in S.W. China (after SKINNER and BERRY).

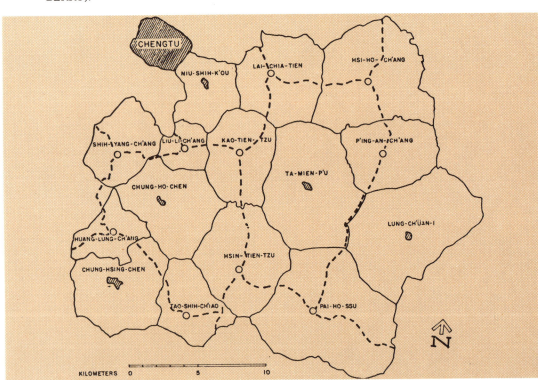

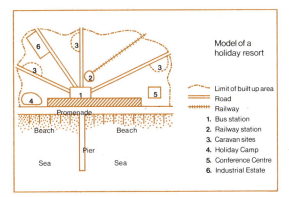

Fig. 2:21 *Model of a holiday resort.*

atic coasts. Resorts can be grouped into sub-types including:

(a) Coastal resorts, e.g. Blackpool, Scarborough, Torbay
(b) Health spas, e.g. Bath, Buxton, Baden Baden (Germany)
(c) Mountain sports resorts for skiing and climbing, e.g. Aviemore, Aspen (Colorado), Cortina D'Ampezzo (Italy), Leysin (Switzerland)
(d) Historical and Cultural centres, e.g. Edinburgh, Salzburg (Austria).

Type (d) are major tourist centres although not strictly resorts in the same way as (a), (b) and (c).

Assignment

4 (a) Figs. 2:21 and 2:22 illustrate two different types of Resorts. Fig. 2:21 shows a typical seaside resort and Fig. 2:22 a typical mountain ski resort. Make a list of the main features of each resort. Which functions are present in the coastal resort and not in the mountain resort? Which are present in the mountain resort and not in the coastal resort?

(b) Why is there a need for the following in the coastal resort: (i) Conference centre; (ii) Caravan site; (iii) Industrial estate?

(c) What facilities could be added to the mountain resort to make it suitable for all year round tourism?

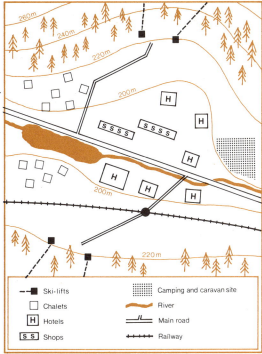

Fig. 2:22 *Model of a ski resort.*

Case Study 5—Bridlington (Fig. 2:23)

This resort is situated on the east coast of Yorkshire, near Flamborough Head some thirty-five kilometres from Scarborough. During the summer season the population rises from about 28 000 to around 100 000. Visitors to the town are catered for by a wide range of retail, transport and entertainment facilities. These include for example, most types of shops, cinemas, bingo halls, a golf course, a long promenade, hotels and public houses, well cared for beaches and a Spa. The Royal Hall which was opened in 1932 now functions as a variety theatre and as a conference centre. It can accommodate up to 2000 people. This can be quite important especially if the town is to attract some trade during the off-peak season. The town also boasts a harbour and a jetty although unlike many, it does not have a pier.

To offset the problems of seasonal unemployment, Bridlington has been trying to attract some industrial development for some time. Several firms have been established recently ranging from textile factories to a distribution point for a major car firm. Other major problems being tackled include efforts to protect the coastal areas from the effects of erosion, longshore drift and pollution. The chalk headland is gradually being eroded and thus large tracts have been fenced off from public use. Similarly, groynes have been built to alleviate the effects of beach erosion. Effluent and sewage and occasionally oil slicks threaten the beaches. A great deal of time, money and effort has been involved quite recently in an attempt to cope with this. Future success may depend greatly upon these efforts.

RELIGIOUS CENTRES

These range from the centre of a faith (Rome, Roman Catholics; Jerusalem, Jews; Mecca, Moslems; Salt Lake City, Mormons) to towns with regional or special religious importance. Cathedral towns are examples of the regional type and places such as Lourdes, Fatima and Bethlehem of the special category associated normally with miracles, visions or particularly important religious events.

Religious centres have several common features such as the importance of religious buildings in the structure of the town and the function of religious administration as a major role of the settlement. All attract visitors or pilgrims although the regional centres are overshadowed by the centres of particular faiths and especially important historical centres (e.g. Lourdes, Bethlehem). Of course, in many large cities the religious function is only part of the total array of activities. Thus Rome is the capital of Italy and a major international commercial city and fashion centre in addition to performing the role of the home of Roman Catholicism. Equally some small settlements may be important religious centres in that they are the site of a cathedral. This function is not clearly correlated with the population size of a centre.

39

40

UNIVERSITY TOWNS

We could make a list of all settlements with a university but the members would not all be university towns in the sense that this particular function is dominant. In most cases the university is only a part of the functional mix but in places such as Oxford, Cambridge, Keele, Lampeter and St. Andrews the number of students amounts to more than one quarter of the total population of the settlement. University buildings form a distinctive portion of the 'morphology' of these towns. More significantly the rhythm of university life affects the economy of the town. During vacations there is a decline in the demand for goods and services in the town unless the university attracts conferences to fill the empty rooms in the student halls of residence. Of course, particularly famous university towns such as Oxford and Cambridge become centres for tourism which adds to the economic success of the settlement. The location of the university within a settlement varies from place to place. Some are sited centrally (Aston in Birmingham and Strathclyde in Glasgow) whereas others have a campus on the outskirts, e.g. Stirling and York. The latter group benefit from additional space for halls of residence and playing fields whereas the centrally located universities have the advantage of accessibility within the urban area to offset possible problems of the availability and cost of space for facilities.

CAPITALS

The predominant function of a capital is administration. Various types of capitals can be identified as the following list illustrates:

1. National Capitals
   (a) Major Cities: These are the capitals of countries and are often the largest city, e.g. London, Paris, Vienna
   (b) Compromise Capitals: These are chosen to avoid conflict between rival major cities, e.g. Washington, Canberra, Ottawa

   (c) Forward Capitals: Chosen to encourage development in less attractive areas, e.g. Brasilia
2. State Capitals, e.g. Munich, Bavaria; Richmond, Virginia
3. Regional Capitals, e.g. Glasgow, Strathclyde; Birmingham, West Midlands.

Assignment
5 What are the distinctive features of: (a) National capitals (b) Regional capitals? For example, you may refer to the tendency of capitals to have many civic buildings such as museums and art galleries. Do these occur in both (a) and (b)?

Fig. 2:24 Model of the industrial structure of a port (J. EVERSON and B. FITZGERALD).

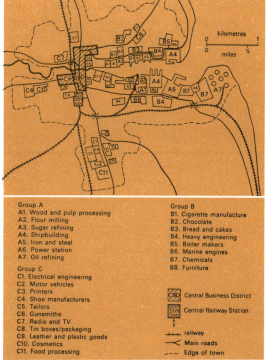

Group A
A1. Wood and pulp processing
A2. Flour milling
A3. Sugar refining
A4. Shipbuilding
A5. Iron and steel
A6. Power station
A7. Oil refining

Group C
C1. Electrical engineering
C2. Motor vehicles
C3. Printers
C4. Shoe manufacturers
C5. Tailors
C6. Gunsmiths
C7. Radio and TV
C8. Tin boxes/packaging
C9. Leather and plastic goods
C10. Cosmetics
C11. Food processing

Group B
B1. Cigarette manufacture
B2. Chocolate
B3. Bread and cakes
B4. Heavy engineering
B5. Boiler makers
B6. Marine engines
B7. Chemicals
B8. Furniture

CBD Central Business District
Stn Central Railway Station
+++ railway
Main roads
--- Edge of town

Opposite – Fig. 2:23 East Yorkshire resort of Bridlington.

PORTS

There are many different types of ports in terms of site and functional structure. Depending on size and precise function, ports normally have various dock and harbour facilities. In addition, industries will be attracted because the port is a 'break of bulk' point where goods are loaded and unloaded. Apart from associated industries such as shipbuilding and repair yards, processing industries include canneries, bottling plants, textile mills and sugar refineries, and bulk storage and handling warehouses, e.g. granaries. Other activities include government offices (customs and excise), insurance and trading companies. Harbour facilities can range from a quay to elaborate sets of docks and specialized handling equipment. A recent feature has been the development of container terminals. Ports specializing in the use of 'container freight' set aside large areas for storing the box-shaped containers. Special lifting equipment is required to move the containers from lorries and railway wagons on to ships. This method simplifies loading and handling of goods, offering savings in time and cost. Goods suffer less damage in transshipment and the possibility of loss is also reduced, since the containers are sealed. It is especially beneficial for shipowners because it means quicker loading and unloading of ships and therefore more trips per year for each ship.

Fig. 2:24 illustrates the range and distribution of industrial premises found in a hypothetical port. The industries are arranged into three groups. Each group tends to seek a different location within the port. Group A industries because of the bulky nature of the imported raw materials require a waterfront location. Group B industries are usually found quite close to the dockland areas since the industries in this group manufacture goods from imported raw materials and therefore seek locations which minimize transportation of the raw materials. The last group consists of light industries which may or may not be associated with the first two groups. Consequently, their location pattern is less restricted and industrial premises may be more scattered throughout the city area.

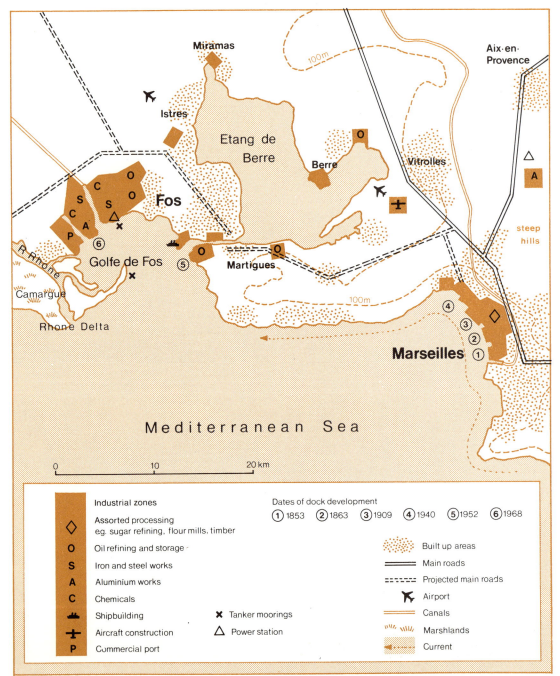

Industrial zones

◇ Assorted processing
 e.g. sugar refining, flour mills, timber

O Oil refining and storage

S Iron and steel works

A Aluminium works

C Chemicals

⚓ Shipbuilding

✈ Aircraft construction

P Commercial port

✕ Tanker moorings

△ Power station

Dates of dock development

① 1853 ② 1863 ③ 1909 ④ 1940 ⑤ 1952 ⑥ 1968

Built up areas

Main roads

Projected main roads

✈ Airport

Canals

Marshlands

◄ Current

Case Study 6—Marseilles Port Complex (Figs. 2:25, 26 and 27)

Founded by the Greeks over 2000 years ago, Marseilles owes its growth to the trade which developed during the nineteenth-century period of colonial expansion. Trade with African colonies, the Middle East and the Far East enabled this port to expand and become France's main port and second city after Paris. Imports include oil, tropical produce (cocoa, coffee, sugar cane) and iron ore. In order to cope with the huge supertankers bringing vast quantities of oil, out-port developments were constructed on the shores of the Etang de Berre and Etang de Fos to the west of the city. Recent industrial developments in this area include large petro-chemical works and oil refineries which have been added to the complex range of port industries and the steel-making mill. As the port continues to expand, more pressure is being felt from the accommodation needs of the population. Several major projects have been initiated recently to build new housing and to rebuild older sectors of the city. New shopping centres and office blocks have also been built as part of this redevelopment programme. Further expansion, however, is limited by the lack of available building space due to the fact that the city is encircled to the north by hills such as the Chaine de L'Etoile. Some have called Marseilles the 'Europort of Southern Europe'. This may be a slight exaggeration since the port lacks the number and variety of industries of its Dutch counterpart.

6 Study the map of Marseilles and Etang de Fos Fig. 2:25. List the main industries present in the Etang de Fos area. How does the range of industry differ from that shown in the hypothetical port in Fig. 2:24? Can you account for these apparent differences, e.g. perhaps refer to size factor; exports/imports; locations, etc.

Fig. 2:25 Marseilles-Fos port complex (after RANDLE).

Fig. 2:26 *The port of Marseilles. Docks, warehouses and a yacht marina front the buildings of the city centre.*

Fig. 2:27 *The port of Marseilles. The breakwater gives protection to shipping in the harbour. The docks give additional space for loading and unloading. Note the power station, the oil storage tanks, the railway sidings and the various industries and warehouses.*

Classification by Settlement Size

The main problem we face when grouping settlements according to size is that of choosing an appropriate indicator of 'size'. The most commonly used indicator is population size. Settlements vary from single farmsteads to huge urban areas with populations numbering in the millions, e.g. Sao Paulo (8 million), Calcutta (7 million). Certain terms have been used to describe settlements within different size ranges. These include: Dispersed farmstead; hamlet; village; minor town; major town; city; city region; millionaire city.

We discussed the variation in definition of some terms in Chapter 1. What constitutes a village for example in England with a population of about 2000, may in fact be identified as a town in the Mid-West of the United States. The term millionaire city can cover a wide variety of population sizes, from one million up to eleven million persons.

The world's major conurbations include the Ruhr of West Germany, the Randstad of Holland, the Paris Basin, the Detroit-Cleveland and Pittsburg areas of the United States, the West Midlands and Greater London areas of Britain. The northeastern seaboard of the United States between Boston and Washington has been described as a megalopolis. The same term could be applied to the area on the west coast of the U.S.A. from San Francisco to Los Angeles. It has been suggested that in Europe the conurbations of Holland, Belgium, Northern France and the Ruhr might one day merge to form one vast urban complex on the same scale as that of the east coast of the U.S.A. on the basis of commuter patterns, networks of movement of goods and population density. In Japan, Tokyo, Yokohama, Nagoya, Kyoto, Osaka and Kobe merge to form the megalopolis known as Tokaido.

Lewis Mumford used the term Megalopolis in a different way to describe a condition of decay in which material wealth was supposed to dominate life in a city area and 'big was beautiful'. Art was replaced by vulgarity in terms of the size and style of buildings and the evils of bureaucracy became increasingly evident. Whether this is true of the areas mentioned above is debatable. However, the control of public amenities and the administration of such vast urban complexes creates many problems. Cities such as New York and possibly London are approaching this state. We will return to the problems of urban areas in Chapter 5.

Site and Situation

Site is associated with the actual ground on which a settlement is built. Situation refers to the more general relationship of the settlement to other settlements, transport routes and other geographical features. The choice of site is influenced by physical and human factors including:

(a) Local relief features such as the topography of the site which may offer particular attractions for settlements, e.g. a flat site near a river. There is often a situational component in the evaluation of a site.

(b) Local geological factors such as permeable and impermeable rock or fertile and infertile soil

(c) Local drainage features including rivers, springs and lakes

(d) Access to water transport

(e) The need for defence and protection and the desire for strategic advantages

(f) The presence of local sources of raw materials such as coal, iron ore or timber

(g) Advantages accruing from local accessibility.

You may have gathered that site of a settlement can influence the functional character, e.g. factors (d) and (f) may be linked with the emergence of settlements as trade and industrial centres, whilst factor (a) is important in the development of functional types such as seaside resorts where the coastal site becomes a resource for the development of the settlement. In most cases however, it is the situation factors which often supersede the site factors in terms of the pattern of growth, development and eventual functional character of the settlement. Trade links with other settlements will encourage growth but the links greatly depend on the 'nodality' or accessibility of the settlement relative to other settlements in the region. Thus settlements which are centrally located or are built in areas with good road, rail or sea connections to other areas have a tremendous situational advantage. The growth and eventual importance of Paris for example owes much to its central situation in France.

Classification based on Site and Situation

When settlements are classified on this basis, the following terms are commonly used:

(a) River sites
(b) Coastal sites
(c) Gap sites and sites on constricted routeways
(d) Bridging points and heads of navigation
(e) Wet points and dry point sites
(f) Defence sites
(g) Frontier situations
(h) Central situations
(i) Resource situations.

The next section outlines briefly some of the more important aspects of settlements in the above categories.

RIVER SITES

The need for water may be the original reason for the establishment of a settlement on a river site. However, if the river is wide and deep enough it might eventually serve as an important means of communication for the movement of passenger and freight transport, e.g. Ouse (York), Seine (Paris) and Rhine (Cologne). Many ports have developed on river estuaries including London on the Thames, Newcastle on the Tyne and Glasgow on the Clyde. River deltas are also notable locations for the development of major ports such as Rotterdam (Rhine delta) and Marseilles (Rhone delta). Other river sites include confluence points which like estuarine sites are really a sub-category within this particular group. Towns such as Grangemouth (Carron and Forth), Lyons (Rhone and Saone), Mainz (Rhine and Necker) and Kuala Lumpur (Klang and Gombak) took advantage of this situational opportunity.

COASTAL SITES

The development of these sites is closely related to the type of coastline. Rias with their deep water channels and gently rolling landscapes offer attractive sites for the development of major oil terminals. Huge oil tankers can dock safely and cargoes can be easily dispatched to their destinations since the local relief does not seriously impede communications. Milford Haven in south-west Wales is a striking example of one such development which has become an important British oil terminal.

Wide coastal plains with long, sandy beaches are very suitable for the development of resorts. Many resorts border the Spanish and French Mediterranean coasts. Other kinds of settlement attracted to coastal sites obviously include fishing villages. They often seek sheltered harbours on fiorded or ria coastlines.

GAP TOWNS

The chief reason why this particular position is chosen for settlement is usually because the settlement is able to enjoy the advantage of commanding the routes which pass through a major gap or pass between two or more ranges of hills or mountains. Examples include Guildford (England), Innsbruck (Austria), Delhi (India) and Kabul (Afghanistan). Settlements also develop at points where there is severe constriction of routeways such as at rapids on a river, a gorge or a narrowing of straits on a main waterway. Such towns command strategic locations which often explains their initial economic growth. Copenhagen on the narrow sound between Denmark and Sweden and Istanbul situated on the Dardanelles Channel are good examples.

BRIDGING POINTS

Places which allow control over the lower bridging points on important rivers are attractive sites. Many such settlements subsequently became important trading centres. Often the name of the town betrays its origin, e.g. Oxford, Cambridge and Bradford. Other settlements have chosen sites which mark the highest point of navigation of a major river, e.g. Montreal on the St. Lawrence.

WET POINT AND DRY POINT SITES

Many villages occupy spring line sites at the base of chalk or limestone escarpments to be near a source of fresh water. Typical examples are found in the areas at the foot of the Marlborough Downs and the base of the limestone escarpment of the Cotswolds. These settlements are often called settlements on **wet point** sites. The opposite of these are those settlements which are sited on higher ground above marshlands, e.g. the Fen-land villages of Lincolnshire and Norfolk. They are referred to as **dry point** sites.

DEFENCE SITES

The chief factors governing the selection of sites in this case are the desire for protection coupled with the desire to take advantage of the strategic value of the site. Hill lands offered protection against enemy attack and were extremely suitable for the building of forts and castles, e.g. Quebec, Edinburgh and Stirling. The strategic value of command over major routeways or gaps, as for example in the case of Jerusalem and Athens were good reasons for establishing settlements at these points. In the case of castle towns, early settlement growth often occurred downwards from the castle. In Edinburgh for instance where the castle is sited on a crag, early growth occurred along the tail.

Several other settlements have developed as important garrison towns and naval and air bases. The choice of site here was governed by the need for a strategic, sheltered position with access to perhaps road, rail and water transport. These settlements provide training facilities and barracks for the armed forces. Examples include the army town of Aldershot, the naval bases at Portsmouth and Rosyth and the air base at Leuchars in Scotland. At one time there were numerous British bases scattered across the Empire, e.g. Singapore and Malta. The precise site requirements vary depending upon the dominant use of the base (army, navy, air force) but they tend to have common characteristics such as security and the availability of a sufficient amount of land which can primarily, or exclusively, be devoted to use by the armed services.

FRONTIER TOWNS

These settlements have developed on sites on the border of two distinct regions. These regions may be physical, e.g. natural regions or different areas of relief, or possibly be different in their levels of economic and social development. The frontier town is therefore able to enjoy the advantage of obtaining goods from both areas whilst simultaneously serving both as a trade centre.

Towns situated on the border between desert and savanna areas such as Timbuktu and Kano have developed into lively trade centres and transshipment points for people moving along the desert's edge and across the desert. The junction of two distinct regions (mountains and plain) attract settlement. Their situational advantage stimulates trade. There are many examples of important settlements in this category including Como in northern Italy and Hanover and Dresden on the southern edge of the North German Plain.

Pioneer settlements occur at the junction of developed and under-developed areas, marking the furthest point of 'civilization'. Some pioneer settlements are comparatively well organized, highly developed communities in contrast to the simple homesteads in the less developed regions. In the U.S.S.R. and Brazil attempts have been made to encourage people to move into the more difficult environments of Siberia and the Mato Grosso by establishing completely new major settlements such as Verkhoyansk and Brasilia. However, it is the unplanned settlements which correspond more closely to the image of frontier towns which you gain from 'Western' pictures. They offer a simple range of facilities and the buildings make extensive use of readily available local building materials.

SETTLEMENTS IN CENTRAL SITUATIONS

Market towns owe much of their development to their nodal or central locations. These settlements are well situated in relation to their surrounding areas which they serve and are highly accessible by road and in most cases by rail. Many settlements in similar situations have taken advantage of this accessibility factor to grow into important trade and commercial centres, industrial and communication centres. We have already mentioned how Paris took advantage of its situation and has become the capital and first city of France. Fig. 2:28 shows the location of Paris and illustrates the advantages which the city derives from being located at the centre of France's major road and railway networks. The city in fact acts like a magnet drawing trade and people into the centre. This pattern is repeated with many cities throughout the world including, for example, Chicago in the Mid-West of the U.S.A. which enjoys good road, rail and water communications with the rest of the country. A slightly different situation occurs with Singapore, which although not centrally located within the country is nevertheless highly central to other countries and major cities in South-East Asia.

RESOURCE SITUATIONS

Obvious examples are mining settlements. However, if we extend the definition of resource to include any environmental property which is of economic value to man and likely to attract settlement then many types of sites and situations would come into this category.

Conclusion

We have shown that settlements can be grouped according to certain basic features, often irrespective of the regions in which the settlements are located. From these classifications we can also identify certain underlying forces and patterns which govern the growth, development and functional character of settlements. No classification can be claimed inevitably better than another. The usefulness greatly depends upon the purpose and intent of the study. If we appreciate the factors involved in the choice of settlement site and the evolution of functional character of settlements in general, we gain valuable insight into the complex processes involved in this facet of man's response to his environment. It is in this wider context that the study of settlements and the attempts to derive classification systems perhaps makes its most valuable contribution to geographical study.

Revision Questions

1   Why do geographers classify settlements?
2   Make a list of the functions of settlements.
3   Which functions are usually referred to in studies dealing with service centres?
4   What do you understand by the concept of 'a hierarchy of Central Places'?
5   Which functions would you expect to find in a market town which would not be found in a resort? Which functions would you expect to find in a resort which would not be found normally in a market town?
6   In what ways are resorts and university towns similar in respect of seasonal population changes? How do they differ in this respect?
7   How would coastal/seaside resorts differ from mountain resorts in terms of: (a) functions (b) seasonal rates of occupation?
8   How would the functions of an all year round mountain resort differ from a winter sports resort?
9   Outline the chief functions of a major port.
10   What are container terminals? Briefly list the chief advantages of this type of freight carrying over more traditional methods.
11   Which factors are most responsible for the siting of the following types of settlement: a castle town; a port; a spring line settlement; a resort; a mining town.
12   How is site and situation related to functional character? Illustrate your answer by referring to any examples of settlements known to you.

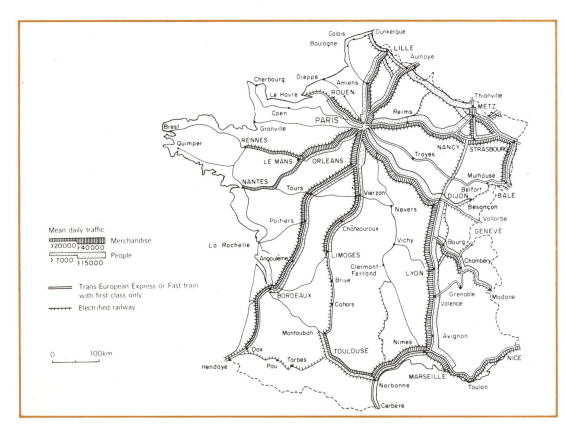

Fig. 2:28 *The French rail network illustrates the centrality of Paris (J. BEAUJEU-GARNIER).*

8 Study Fig. 2:29. Write a brief description of the main features shown on this photograph.

9 (a) Write notes on the port features shown in Fig. 2:30.

(b) List the principal differences between the port installations shown in Figs. 2:29 and 2:30.

(c) List the principal differences between the port features shown in Fig. 2:27 and those in Fig. 2:30.

Page 47   Fig. 2:29
Oil installations, Europoort.

Fig. 2:30
The West German river port of Duisburg.

CHAPTER THREE
SETTLEMENTS AND THEIR HINTERLANDS

When we discussed the function of service centres in Chapter 2, we noted that these settlements served not only their resident populations but also many people living in the area surrounding the settlement. The study of the precise nature of that surrounding region in terms of its size, shape and general relationship with the centre serving it forms the second major component of Central Place Theory. Various terms have been coined to describe this surrounding region. These include — Hinterland, Sphere of Influence, Urban Field, Service Area, Trade Area and Complementary Region. The last term is the one used by Christaller in his study of settlements in Southern Germany.

Although these terms mean approximately the same thing, they are not exactly similar. We tend to use the term **hinterland** when we refer mainly to the area served by a large city, town or port. For example London's hinterland extends throughout the whole of Britain and for a specialist centre such as Oxford the university town, the hinterland could be regarded as encompassing most of the countries of the world. We need to recognize therefore the difference between these kinds of hinterlands, which are either large or very specialized, and those more compact hinterlands of Central Places. We will develop this point later in this chapter. In the case of a port, hinterland describes the area or zone from which the port obtains its supplies of goods for export and the area throughout which it distributes its imported goods. For example, the hinterland of the Rotterdam-Europoort complex extends throughout many countries including Holland, West Germany, France and Switzerland. Goods such as oil are imported into Holland from Rotterdam's **foreland**. The foreland consists of those countries which export to Holland. Once imported the goods are distributed throughout the countries listed above.

We must recognize one important fact, namely, that the general hinterland of a settlement consists of several different hinterlands and the boundary of the general hinterland is really a zone made up of the boundaries of these hinterlands. Each relates to a particular good or service being distributed from the centre. Thus, from Rotterdam, a commodity such as oil can be distributed over a very wide area whereas imported raw materials for the textile industry may be distributed over a much smaller region. Similarly, in a city, the service area for a large city hospital may extend over an extremely large area, especially if the hospital offers specialized treatment. By contrast, the newspaper circulation area for an evening newspaper within the same city might be spread over a smaller region. Canniesburn Hospital in Glasgow takes patients from all over Scotland since it specializes in plastic surgery whereas the local evening newspaper in the same city — the *Evening Times* — is circulated to people living within the boundary of approximately one hour's commuting distance by road or rail. These illustrate our point. It is quite obvious therefore that the size and shape of hinterlands are governed by several different factors.

One of the most important of these factors is the nature and scope of **transportation** within the region. If an area is well suited to the development of an integrated system of road and rail transport, then the movement of goods throughout that area is made much easier. Imported goods can be distributed over a much wider area and the urban centre can obtain goods more easily if it is accessible to the surrounding region. In effect, the size of the hinterland will often increase. Alternatively, if anything disrupts the accessibility factor, such as the presence of mountainous relief or the imposition of a political frontier, the size and shape of the hinterland can be seriously impaired. When for example, Germany was split into two separate countries at the end of World War II, the hinterland of the port of Hamburg was considerably changed. It no longer had access to the areas lying to the east. East Germany began to trade with the communist bloc countries and was effectively removed from Hamburg's hinterland. The port was thus forced to develop increased trading activity with the areas to the south and west, notably the Ruhr and Westphalian districts of West Germany.

A second factor affecting the extent of a hinterland is that of population density. Many ports and cities are considered to have fairly large hinterlands when the hinterlands are measured strictly in terms of areal size (sq. kms). However, when the total number of people living within these hinterlands is considered the situation becomes more complex. If the population density is low, then the hinterland in terms of collection and distribution of goods may not be as important as one where the population density is much higher. Given a larger number of people, the volume and variety of trade may correspondingly increase. When the population is scarce, this volume and variety might be seriously curtailed. Much depends upon the type of goods being handled by the port. If the port specializes in particular commodities such as the export of iron ore, oil or bauxite, then the volume of trade handled can be extremely high despite the fact that there are relatively few people living in the hinterland. This is true of ports such as Abadan in Iran, Kiruna in Sweden and Weipa in North Queensland, Australia, which were created to deal with the demand for a base from which to export their products.

On a similar note, if the hinterland consists of a highly industrialized area, the importance of that hinterland will be much greater. For instance, New York's hinterland which includes the Appalachian coalfield and the steel centres of Pittsburg and Detroit is extremely important because of this. The volume of trade in terms of raw materials and finished products handled by New York is immense. The variety and complexity of the trade is also much greater than in the case of a port handling one or two agricultural products such as coffee or grain. In effect therefore the economic landscape influences the importance of the hinterland.

In many instances the hinterland can also be affected by the functional character of the settlement. Those settlements which offer specialized functions such as Resort or Educational functions may have hinterlands far greater than their population size or overall total number of service facilities might otherwise suggest. The county town of Ayr for example, has a population of approximately 48 000 and offers a fairly extensive range of retail, wholesale and service establishments, including outlets of Marks and Spencer, Boots and Woolworth. The range and variety of these establishments is as much as one might expect to find in a town of this size. However, the hinterland of the Ayr cattle market stretches from the county of Dumfries in the south to as far north as Perth. Furthermore, the holiday resort function of the town attracts many visitors from all parts of Scotland throughout the summer months. Therefore in towns such as Ayr, the specialization factor has important repercussions so far as the extent of different types of hinterlands are concerned. These hinterlands reflect the importance of the particular product, service or specialism being offered. Thus in the case of resorts, the attractiveness of the settlement affects the size of the area over which it has influence. Similarly, in a University Town, the hinterland is influenced by the ability of that settlement to provide a very highly specialized educational service, and so attract students from a very large area.

When Walter Christaller examined the relationship in Southern Germany between the centres and the areas which these centres served, he ignored all functions except the service or Central Place functions of the settlements. In other words he confined his work to the study of the nature of the shape and size of the hinterlands of the service activities in his Central Places. This is in essence the difference between the concept of hinterland in the wider context of large industrial and commercial cities and ports and that of the sphere of influence or complementary regions of a Central Place system. Nevertheless, the same situation whereby the trade area or sphere of influence of a Central Place consists of several rather than one single area, which we mentioned earlier, still pertains. When we refer to a settlement as having a trade area, in fact the boundary of that trade area is an arbitrary boundary drawn from data relating to the boundaries of several Central Place functions. Functions such as newsagents, cleaner's service and department stores, which can be broadly grouped into low, middle and high order functions, draw customers from different areas. Sometimes the boundaries of these areas coincide, but often what emerges is that, as a rule, the higher the order of the Central Place function, the larger the trade area of that function. This relationship is examined in more detail later. For the moment we will consider the question of whether the shape of trade areas conforms to any sort of pattern and if so, what factors generate the pattern.

The Shape of Trade Areas

In Chapter 2 reference was made to the concept of a hierarchy of Central Places related to different orders of goods provided by different orders of Central Places. These centres are spaced out on the landscape, under perfect conditions, in a completely regular manner with equal distances between centres of equal service importance. To achieve this situation we would require a flat plain, an even distribution of population, equality of transport in all directions and the absence of any distorting influences. Under these conditions, a geometrically structured pattern of service centres would occur with a large number of villages and a small number of cities, each carefully and regularly located to produce a perfectly spaced pattern. This would also apply to the shape of the trade areas of the different orders of Central Places.

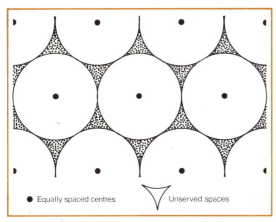

Fig. 3:1 Circular trade areas result in unserved spaces.

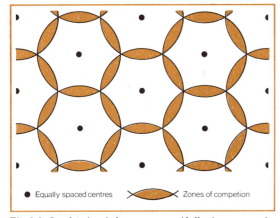

Fig. 3:2 Overlapping circles are necessary if all points are served.

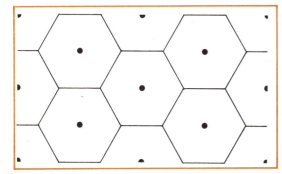

Fig. 3:3 Hexagons give a perfect solution, no duplication occurs and nowhere is unserved.

In theory, one would expect that the trade areas of service centres would have an approximately circular shape as shown in Fig. 3:1. In this situation we assume that the Central Places are all of equal size and distributed in a regularly spaced pattern. You will notice that between the circles there are areas of unserved spaces. If we adjust the distribution of the Central Places, so that they are closer, then the situation in Fig. 3:2 pertains. Here the trade areas overlap. In the shaded areas the settlements compete with each other. If we can assume that this zone of competition is shared equally between the centre and its neighbour, we can draw lines through the competition zones bisecting them. This leads to a pattern of hexagonal trade areas as in Fig. 3:3. This is the most efficient way in which the centres can serve the populations of their surrounding regions. We must remember, however, that this is a theoretical pattern based on several assumptions which may not always be found in reality.

One important assumption which is made is that of equal access in all directions. This implies that consumers living within the study areas are able to reach all of the centres with the same amount of ease. No allowance is therefore made for the nature of the relief of the area, yet the presence of an area of hill land could affect the nature of communications within the area. Similarly, movement could be affected by the quality and frequency of public transport services. When these and other factors relating to accessibility are taken into account, the shape of the trade areas can be altered considerably. They may become distended in various directions as shown in Fig. 3:4.

Another important consideration is that of how the centres in the study area are distributed. If they are regularly spaced then the patterns may conform generally to that suggested in Fig. 3:3. In many cases as several studies have shown, the only areas where you are likely to find settlements regularly distributed are those which are generally flat and agricultural. These areas are often less complicated in terms of their communications patterns and distribution of population. It is significant that many of the studies which confirmed the notions of regular distribution patterns were

undertaken in areas such as Wisconsin, Iowa, South-West England and Southern Germany. These areas are largely rural and agricultural in character. When the patterns of trade areas were studied in more complex industrial regions, the spatial distribution pattern of the settlements was also found to be far more complex. For a variety of reasons, many settlements of the same size were found to be located quite close to one another. This obviously disrupted the theoretical patterns suggested by Central Place Theory.

Another important assumption is that the populations of the trade areas are evenly distributed. In reality, this rarely happens. Once again it is more likely to occur in areas with a rural rather than an industrial background. It is also assumed that if consumers in the surrounding areas of service centres have equal ease of access to centres in their area and the centres offer the same range of goods and services then these consumers will wish to shop in the nearest centre which offers their desired purchase. This is why we would expect to have circular or hexagonal trade areas. The decision making of where to shop is thus affected by **distance minimization**. However, this does not always happen. Consumers do not always make a choice of shopping area on simple

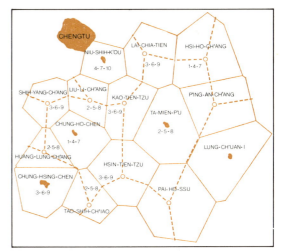

Fig. 3:4 Distended trade areas in Szechwan, China (B. BERRY).

distance from their home. Their decision making may be affected by other things including for example, whether or not they own a car, how attractive they consider one centre is as opposed to another, how much it costs in terms of time or money to shop in different centres, how good the parking facilities are or indeed where they work. All of the assumptions made with regard to the theoretical shape of trade areas of Central Places can be brought together under the general term **Homogeneous Landscape**, which is applied to the whole area under study. However, as we have seen in reality few areas are homogeneous. There are many variations in terms of the physical and human landscapes which can disturb the expected patterns.

One question which springs to mind is 'how are the theoretical patterns affected by variations in the size of the Central Place and the size of trade areas?' As we showed earlier, the centres in a Central Place system are grouped into a series of different orders ranging from low to high order centres. Many research studies have shown that

there is a direct relationship between the importance of a Central Place and the size of its trade area. This relationship is illustrated in Fig. 3:5. This has been found to be true of areas such as County Tipperary, East Yorkshire, Wisconsin and South Wales. Christaller measured the size of the trade areas in terms of (a) population and (b) area in square kms. These are shown in Fig. 3:6. In fact what Christaller and many subsequent studies have suggested is that as well as having a 'hierarchy of Central Places', we should also have

Type of Central Place	Population of Service Area	Size of Service Area (Km²)
M	3,500	44
A	11,000	133
K	35,000	400
B	100,000	1,200
G	350,000	3,600
P	1,000,000	10,800
L	3,500,000	32,400

Fig. 3:6 Tabulation of k = 3 system proposed by W. CHRISTALLER.

Fig. 3:5 Maximum size of trade areas of villages, towns and cities on the basis of a study in Iowa (B. BERRY).

Fig. 3:7 The settlement hierarchy of S.W. Iowa.

a **hierarchy of spheres of influence**, as described in Fig. 3:7. The important point here is that the trade areas of smaller centres are located *within* the trade areas of the larger centres. In theory, these should be arranged in a series of hexagons as we discussed earlier. At the lower end of the hierarchy the smaller centres have their own hexagonal market areas. The market area of the next order of settlement overlaps the market areas of the preceding order. Christaller suggested that as a rule each higher order centre would have a one third share in the custom of the lower order centre. In the hexagonal arrangement there are six lower order centres surrounding the next order of centre. This higher order settlement would therefore serve an area equivalent to three of the lower orders. This is made up by adding $\frac{1}{3} + \frac{1}{3} + \frac{1}{3} + \frac{1}{3} + \frac{1}{3} + \frac{1}{3} + 1 = 3$. This is illustrated in Fig. 3:8. This would mean that in effect the market area of a town would be three times the size of the market area of a village. Similarly the market area of a city would be nine times that of the village and so on. He called this the 'rule of three's' and described it as the 'Marketing Principle' where k = 3, i.e. the size of market area always varies by a ratio of 3. The pattern which he derived is shown in Fig. 3:9. Christaller was well aware that this was a very rigid system and that it

Fig. 3:8 The basis of the Market Principle where k = 3.

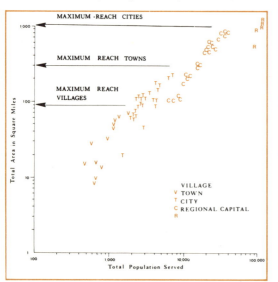

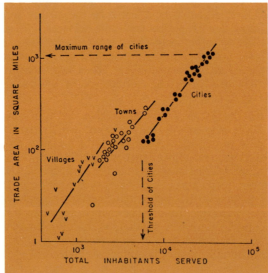

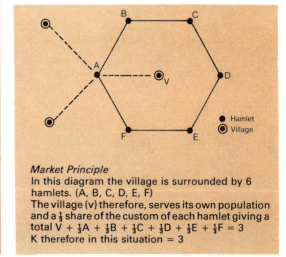

Market Principle
In this diagram the village is surrounded by 6 hamlets. (A, B, C, D, E, F)
The village (v) therefore, serves its own population and a $\frac{1}{3}$ share of the custom of each hamlet giving a total $V + \frac{1}{3}A + \frac{1}{3}B + \frac{1}{3}C + \frac{1}{3}D + \frac{1}{3}E + \frac{1}{3}F = 3$
K therefore in this situation = 3

would be quite difficult to find it in reality. He recognized that, for example, centres located on major transport routes and centres whose prime function was administration could have quite different patterns. He described these alternative patterns as being based upon the Transportation and Administrative Principles in which k = 4 and k = 7 respectively. These are shown in Figs. 3:10 and 3:11.

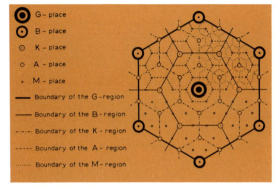

Fig. 3:9 *The hexagonal pattern of the Market Principle.*

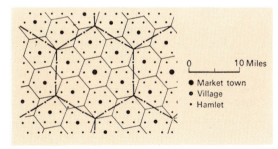

Fig. 3:10 *The hexagonal pattern of the Administrative Principle.*

Fig. 3:11 *The hexagonal pattern of the Transport Principle.*

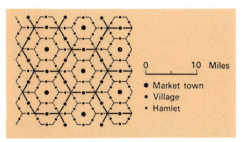

In fact very few studies have been able to show patterns which conform exactly to a perfect hexagonal network. In the real world centres are not distributed evenly, the relief often varies, consumers do not have equal access in all directions, are not equal in income and therefore do not have equal purchasing power. Fig. 3:12 shows the shape of trade areas of Central Places in Ayrshire. You will notice that the pattern does not generally conform to neat hexagons, but important relationships which the theory suggested do emerge. First, the larger Central Places do have larger trade areas. Second, the trade areas of smaller Central Places are contained within the trade area of the larger centres. This conforms to the nesting pattern suggested by Christaller.

A further point we should note in relation to Fig. 3:12 is that as mentioned previously, the trade

Fig. 3:12 *General pattern of hinterlands in Ayrshire.*

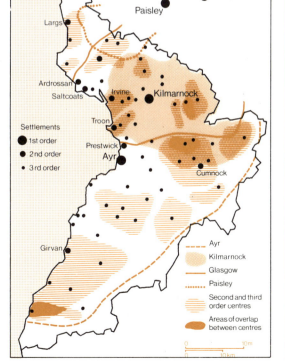

areas of Central Places are really a composite of trade areas of the Central Place functions found within these centres. Each Central Place function has its own sphere of influence from which it draws custom.

For example, if we look at education, a group of primary schools will feed a secondary school so that the primary schools are a low order education function nesting into the higher order service area of the secondary school. We could extend this up the hierarchy and suggest that many secondary schools would be required to provide the student population of a university. This situation can be applied to most goods and services and confirms the concept of a **hierarchy of Central Place functions** which is implicit in Central Place Theory. Fig. 3:13 shows an example of this nesting pattern and is taken from a study of a Central Place system in Ayrshire.

Fig. 3:13 *The nesting of trade areas in Ayrshire.*

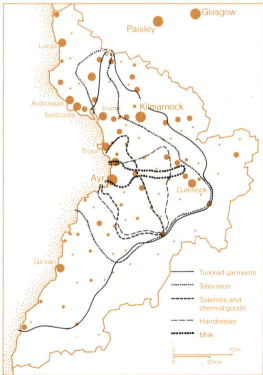

Assignment

1 Go into your local town and make a list of the different types of retail/wholesale and service establishments present in the central area. Select three shops and one service activity (all of different size) and on a suitable day, interview about fifteen customers outside each shop in turn. Ask each customer where they live.

Once you have gathered all the information, plot the origins of each customer for each shop on a blank map of the region. Draw a boundary representing each different shop type. Examine your maps and describe your results. Ask yourself how the trade areas of the larger shops compare to those of the smaller units. Do the trade areas of the smaller units lie within those of the larger ones? If so, what does this reveal?

The study of spheres of influence may seem to you to be largely theoretical and academic, especially in view of what we said about comparisons between the theoretical patterns and the real world. However, this topic of Central Place studies does have its practical uses. Apart from providing us with a model or standard situation from which we can compare settlements in the real world, its value has been well recognized by commercial enterprises. Any business wishing to establish an enterprise in a town can use the principles of the theory to gauge the potential market area for its goods and services. Many large shopping chains such as Woolworths and Marks and Spencer can use the theory to determine which towns would be the best places to establish a network of their stores throughout a country or a region. The spheres of influence may also have important uses for administrative and political purposes. For example, the local government regions which were set up in the early 1970s in Scotland were closely linked to the idea of the 'city region'. In effect most of these regions are based on the field of influence of major towns and cities in Scotland, as Fig. 3:14 shows. Strathclyde Region for instance is based on the general sphere of influence of Glasgow, Lothian Region on Edinburgh, Grampian on Aberdeen and Tayside

on Dundee. Other practical uses include the choice of sites for new hospitals and sports centres in order to serve the optimum population by choosing the most convenient central point for the intended service hinterland. This involves not only studying the necessary level of use of the facility to make it viable but the distribution of population and transport facilities in order to calculate the probable service hinterland.

Delimiting Spheres of Influence

Geographers have used many different methods in their attempts to delimit the boundaries of spheres of influence. Several studies have been based on the use of certain specified indicators. The most commonly used indicators include:

PUBLIC TRANSPORT SERVICES

The study of bus-timetables of local bus services in England, Wales and Northern Ireland was used as a basis for the determination of a town's

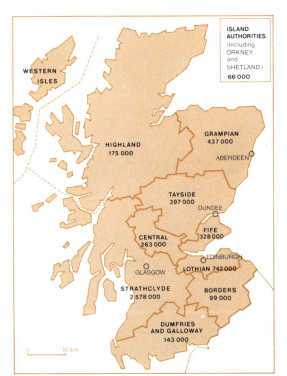

hinterland by F. H. W. Green in the late 1930s. A series of studies continuing through the 1940s and 1950s produced maps showing the pattern of hinterlands of towns in Britain. The more widespread use of the motor car in later years however has complicated the movements of consumers and has obviously affected the value of using this particular indicator. Fig. 3:15 illustrates the patterns found by Green.

NEWSPAPER CIRCULATION

The circulation network of local district newspapers has also been used as an indicator of the extent of the sphere of influence of the settlement in which they are published. Information can be obtained either directly from the newspaper offices, or from the newspaper itself, for instance by inspection of the property for sale sections, local reports and local advertisements. One problem which emerges is that of ensuring that the newspaper is one which operates at a local level and is not a national paper, sold throughout the country. Fig. 3:16 illustrates the hinterlands which were found in New York and Boston (1949).

DELIVERY AREAS OF RETAIL ESTABLISHMENTS

Many large stores, especially department stores keep a record of the addresses of their account customers. If this information is obtained, it can provide a realistic guide to the general trade area from which that particular store draws its custom. Alternatively, if a check is made on where the store's delivery vans operate, this also provides a fairly accurate account of the trade area. The most common problems associated with the use of this particular indicator include, the question of availability of data since many stores will be reluctant to release this kind of information, the need to obtain information from more than one establishment, the effect of out of town shopping centres and hypermarkets, and the impact of journey to work patterns on shopping habits. All of these can affect the precision of this indicator.

Fig. 3:14 Local government regions of Scotland.

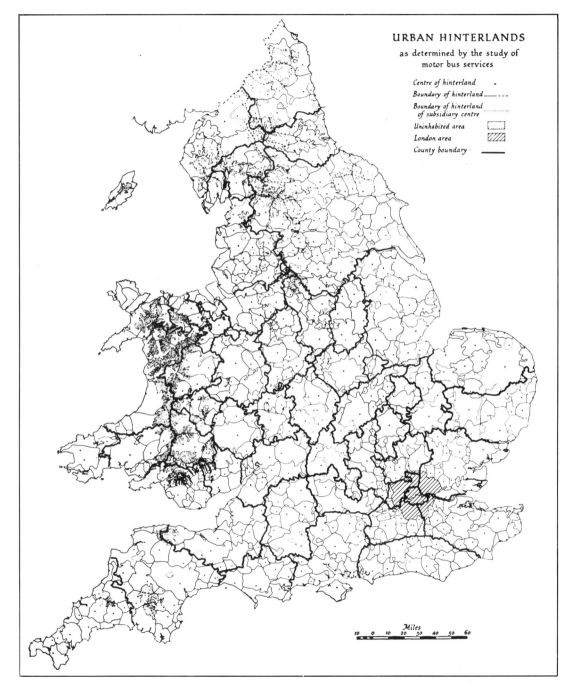

URBAN HINTERLANDS

as determined by the study of
motor bus services

Centre of hinterland	.
Boundary of hinterland	_____
Boundary of hinterland of subsidiary centre	....
Uninhabited area	
London area	
County boundary	———

Miles
10 0 10 20 30 40 50 60

EDUCATIONAL CATCHMENT AREAS

This type of indicator is of very localized value. School catchment areas are often decided now on the basis of factors outwith the normal spatial principles which affect other Central Place functions. For example, you may not attend the nearest school but one which is zoned for your district. Again political factors may be involved, such as the bussing of children in some North American cities such as Boston to give a mix of different racial groups in schools. These distort the spheres of influence of educational establishments and lessen their reliability as general measures of local service hinterlands.

CONSUMER SHOPPING PATTERNS

Many studies have used data relating to consumer movement patterns to determine the boundaries of trade areas. To obtain the required data it is necessary to undertake some form of survey of the shopping habits of consumers within the study area. This survey can either be carried out at:

(a) The point of origin of the consumer, i.e. where the consumer lives

or

(b) The place where the consumer shops, i.e. the Central Place.

A questionnaire is used to gather information relating to:

1. Where the consumer lives
2. Where he/she purchases various listed goods and services
3. How frequently these goods and services are purchased
4. Information about the length of journey and the cost of the journey
5. Possibly an attempt to ascertain which factors govern their choice of shopping centre, e.g. attractiveness, parking facilities, types of shops, etc.

Careful study of the results of these surveys can produce maps showing what has been described

Fig. 3:15 Trade hinterlands of England and Wales, 1950, defined by bus services (F. H. W. GREEN).

55

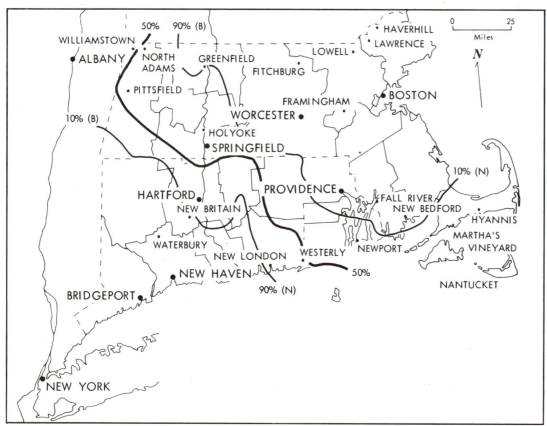

Fig. 3:16 *Newspaper circulation information as a means of hinterland definition. The 50% line means that New York and Boston daily papers have equal volumes of sales and this line approximates to the hinterland boundary between the two cities. Information refers to 1949.*

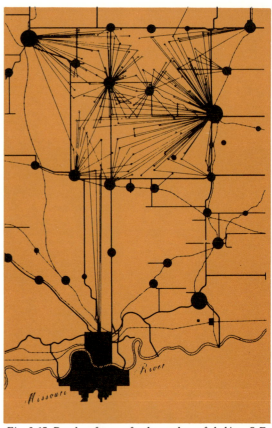

Fig. 3:17 *Rural preferences for the purchase of clothing, S.E. Iowa (B. BERRY). The lines connect place of residence of the consumer to preferred service centre.*

as **Consumer Desire Lines.** Fig. 3:17 shows some examples of consumer patterns in Iowa. Several important points must be observed when using this method. First, the sample needs to be representative of the population. To ensure this, it is important that the survey includes a high response. Persons to be interviewed should be selected randomly. Obviously a 100 per cent survey can rarely be undertaken. The sample however must be large enough to ensure that the occasional unique situation, such as someone on holiday from London who is shopping in York, is

in true proportion. The greater the sample, therefore, the more accurate your results. Secondly, a great deal of thought must be given as to where and when the survey is carried out. Certain days of the week, e.g. Saturdays, may prove better than a mid-week afternoon. Similarly, interviews held outside or at a main shopping area, e.g. a shopping arcade, will give access to a wider variety of consumers. Finally, care should be taken to ensure that the questionnaire is not too long. This can often lead to respondents being unhelpful.

The questions included in the last part of the questionnaire relating to the factors governing choice of centre can be used to explain the shopping patterns. This is especially useful if the patterns of the trade areas differ quite markedly from what you might expect according to the theory. It is little wonder therefore that this area of spheres of influence studies has attracted a great deal of interest from major retail and wholesale companies. Using the techniques which we have briefly outlined above, many commercial businesses make intensive studies of their poten-

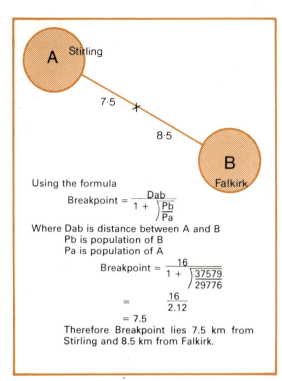

Using the formula

$$\text{Breakpoint} = \frac{Dab}{1 + \sqrt{\dfrac{Pb}{Pa}}}$$

Where Dab is distance between A and B
Pb is population of B
Pa is population of A

$$\text{Breakpoint} = \frac{16}{1 + \sqrt{\dfrac{37579}{29776}}}$$

$$= \frac{16}{2.12}$$

$$= 7.5$$

Therefore Breakpoint lies 7.5 km from Stirling and 8.5 km from Falkirk.

Fig. 3:18 Application of the gravity model to the calculation of the hinterland boundary between Stirling and Falkirk.

tial market areas before committing themselves to setting up an establishment in any particular town.

USE OF THE GRAVITY FORMULA

In contrast to the other methods of determining the boundaries of spheres of influence which are in effect based on data obtained from the real situation, the gravity formula provides a means of theoretically calculating the limits of trade areas. It is based on the idea that a consumer's decision is based generally on the size and importance of the service centre. Size may be measured in terms of population, importance in terms of the total number and variety of Central Place functions located within the centre. The distance a consumer is willing to travel to obtain a good or service should theoretically be directly related to the size of the centre offering that good or service. The formula which was derived by W. Reilly is stated as:

Location of trade boundary between two towns A and B, in Kms from A,

$$\text{is equal to } \frac{\text{Km. between A and B}}{1 + \sqrt{\dfrac{\text{Size of B}}{\text{Size of A}}}}$$

The size of the centres is normally measured by population data. An example of the use of the model is shown in Fig. 3:18, which calculates the break point between Stirling and Falkirk.

We must remember that this formula assumes certain things such as the fact that consumers located in the area between the two towns have equal ease of access to both. Difficulties with public transport, the kinds of roads, physical relief and so on are not taken into account, although they must affect the real situation. In most instances the formula is used as a guide and is often used in conjunction with the results obtained from questionnaire surveys to determine boundaries.

Assignment

2 Visit a large store or newspaper office in your nearest town. Ask the manager if he will assist you by giving you information about where his customers live, or where the store's vans deliver purchased goods, or, where the newspaper circulation area extends.

Plot the information given on a map. Next, calculate the break point between this town and the nearest towns of the same or greater population size. Draw a boundary linking these points on a map. Compare the maps. Does the real situation match the theoretical one? What are the differences? Can you account for these differences?

Two concepts closely associated with the general importance of Central Place functions and their impact on consumer movement within a Central Place region are: (a) Threshhold Population and (b) Range of Goods and Services.

THRESHOLD POPULATION

This term refers to the 'minimum number of people required to support a particular good or service within a Central Place'. You may recall that in Chapter 2 we discussed the concept of a hierarchy of Central Place and the concept of a hierarchy of Central Place functions. We described Central Place functions as belonging to low, middle and high orders. Low order functions were less important than high order ones. It follows that the low order establishments need fewer customers to support them. For example a grocer's shop will require very few customers compared to a large department store like Harrods. Having recognized that minimum thresholds exist, the next problem is that of defining the size of the thresholds for individual functions.

MEASURING THRESHOLD POPULATIONS

Measuring thresholds is not an easy thing to do. For a start, shops vary a great deal in size and in the variety of goods offered for sale. We often use terms such as supermarket (Safeway), variety store (Woolworth), department store (Harrods) to describe shops of a certain type. However, grocers' shops vary in size and even Woolworth's and Safeway's shops are not always exactly similar. Different branches of these stores carry different ranges of goods and there may be some variation in the size. When we try to assess the minimum thresholds for these shops we must be aware of this fact. Several studies have used the technique whereby the range of functions possessed by Central Places are tabulated against the populations of the centres. In effect the population level at which a particular function first affects is taken as a measure of its threshold population. Using this technique, threshold populations were calculated for a group of Central Place functions in Ayrshire in 1974. These are shown in Fig. 3:19. These values may have changed due to demographic growth or decline in that area. If a similar exercise were undertaken in a different part of the country, e.g. Cambridgeshire, we might find slightly different threshold values for each function.

Functional Type	Threshold Value
Marks and Spencer	47,800
Estate Agent	47,800
Theatre	14,000
Travel Agent	14,000
General Furniture Store	12,000
Chartered Surveyors	10,000
Building Society	10,000
Woolworths	7,900
Antiques	5,000
Bank	4,000
Jewellers	3,500
Chemist	1,400
Mini Market	1,300
Cafe	600
Baker	600
General Newsagent	250
Public House	250
Grocer and Provisions	100

Fig. 3:19 An example of the threshold populations for various levels of centre.

Settlement	Population	No. of Shops	Indicator Functions (Number)				
			Banks	Boots the Chemist	Secondary Schools	Marks & Spencer	Auctioneers & Estate Agents
Norwich	120096	1384	33	2	22	1	13
Kings Lynn	27536	433	7	1	6	1	5
Bury	21179	299	5	1	8	1	6
Newmarket	11227	141	2	1	3	0	2
Stowmarket	7795	108	4	1	3	0	2
East Dereham	7199	115	4	1	3	0	1
Wymondham	5904	85	2	0	3	0	1
Thetford	5399	74	3	0	3	0	0
Diss	3681	83	4	0	4	0	3
Swaffham	3202	64	2	0	2	0	0
Downham	2835	74	4	0	0	0	1

Fig. 3:20 Service functions for settlements in the Norwich area (EVERSON and FITZGERALD).

Although this technique is commonly used, it does present problems. First, as we discussed earlier, Central Places serve both their resident populations and a population within a surrounding region. Therefore, it is reasonable to assume that the threshold populations could be greater since the functions would draw custom from both the Central Place and the sphere of influence. This problem has been resolved to some extent by geographers who have shown that the population of a service centre is closely related to the population of the centre plus that of its overall sphere of influence. Thus taking the resident population as an indicator of threshold seems quite reasonable. The second problem occurs if a particular function makes an appearance at an unusual population level. For example, if a supermarket were to appear in a village of about 2000 persons we might question whether it is justified to accept this population as the true threshold population. It may be that the village offers particular advantages, e.g. accessibility linked with building land at low cost to the supermarket. Similarly, some small settlements have banks. These banks however may open only on certain days of the week. Thus we have to use a certain amount of judgement when we come across situations such as these. If the function appears to be a unique occurrence, in most instances we would not accept the population level as a true indication of minimum threshold.

Assignment

3 Refer to Fig. 3:20 above and answer the following questions:
   (a) Find the threshold population for each of the services listed. Are these figures likely to be underestimates?
   (b) Arrange the five indicator functions in hierarchical order and comment on their frequency of occurrence in the table.

RANGE OF GOODS AND SERVICES

We discussed earlier how consumers act so as to minimize the distance which they are prepared to travel in order to obtain a particular good or service. It follows that this distance may increase according to the relative importance of the good or service desired. For example, most people buy convenience goods such as bread, butter and newspapers at their nearest shop. When they wish to make less frequent purchases of more expensive items such as furniture or electrical goods, they may be prepared to travel much further. This distance is defined as the Range of Good or Service. Higher order functions have larger ranges than middle or low order functions. Figs. 3:21 and 3:22 show some examples of the varying ranges of Central Place functions in Iowa.

The range is affected by several factors other than the level of importance of the Central Place function. For a start, various factors as we have seen complicate the decision making of consumers. Many consumers purchase goods in centres which are not always the nearest to them. They may have special preferences for particular centres or perhaps the fact that they work in a particular centre may encourage them to shop there. Indeed, journey to work patterns affect consumer shopping patterns greatly. In terms of the supply side, other factors affecting the range include density of population. For example, the range of goods can be much greater in a rural area than in an urban area. This is because consumers living in an urban area live much closer to their point of purchase. For this and the other factors outlined above, it is often difficult to state precisely what the range of any particular central function might be. Fig. 3:23 illustrates the 'minimum and maximum' ranges of goods in a Central Place system.

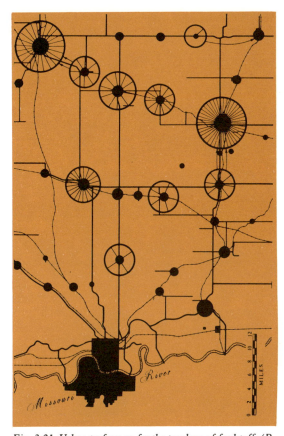

Fig. 3:21 Urban preferences for the purchase of foodstuffs (B. BERRY). Here the consumers live in the service centres.

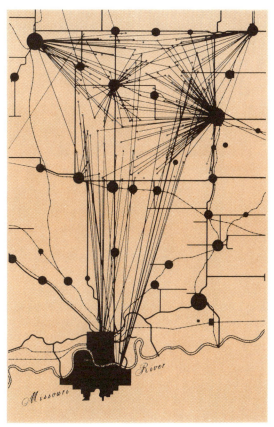

Fig. 3:22 Rural preferences for the purchase of furniture (B. BERRY). Compare this pattern with that shown on Fig. 3:17. Notice the increased importance of the largest settlement for this specialised service (furniture).

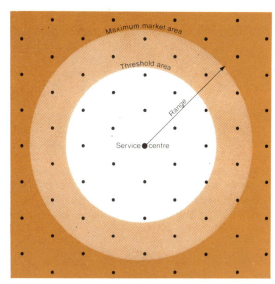

Fig. 3:23 Minimum and maximum range of a good or centre.

Central Place Relationships

We can show that certain relationships exist between Central Places and their hinterlands by correlating the functional status of Central Places with the size of their trade areas. Size may be measured either in terms of area or total population served. This can be done statistically, or by using the scattergraph method as shown in Fig. 3.24. This shows that in this instance a direct relationship exists whereby as the status of the Central Place increases, there is a corresponding increase in the size of the trade area. This rela-

tionship has been studied in several different areas and has been confirmed quite frequently, for example in Ayrshire, Yorkshire and South Wales.

A similar situation can be shown to exist between the functional importance of Central Place functions and their trade areas. Some measure of the importance of individual Central Place functions is required. The centrality index used in many hierarchy studies can be used. This is illustrated in Fig. 3:25 which shows the correlation between Central Place functions and their spheres

of influence in Ayrshire. What is interesting about this particular diagram is the fact that Ayrshire is not entirely rural. The northern part of the country is more industrial in character than the southern part. Bearing in mind what we said earlier about Central Place patterns being perhaps more easily found in rural areas, this pattern in Ayrshire becomes quite significant. However, similar patterns have been found in other industrial and mining areas, notably South Wales.

In conclusion, we have shown that settlements serve not only their resident populations but a wider population contained within a surrounding region. That region is described as the centre's hinterland. We have also seen that so far as Central Places are concerned, these hinterlands should in theory assume certain shapes if they are to ensure that all consumers within the region are being served. The most efficient shape is that of a hexagon. Smaller trade areas of hinterlands exist or nest within the trade areas of larger centres. The shape of the hinterland can be distorted by several different factors. Moreover, the theoretical patterns are most likely to be found in those

59

rural areas in which the relief is limited, thereby approximating to the flat plain assumed in the theory. We have shown that there are definite relationships between the size of hinterlands and the status of both the Central Places and the Central Place functions. We have noted that despite the fact that hinterlands do not always conform to the theoretical patterns suggested in Central Place theory, nevertheless, the model gives us a useful method of comparing the function and distribution of settlements in different areas. Furthermore, the methods employed in the study of Central Places have had many practical implications for commercial, political and administrative purposes.

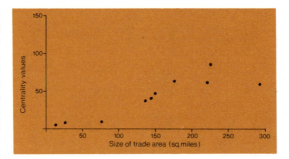

Fig. 3:25 Relationship between central place functions and trade areas.

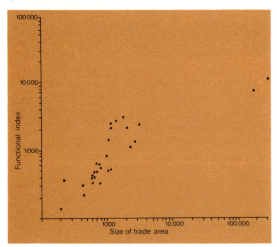

Fig. 3:24 The relationship between the functional index of settlements and the population of their trade areas.

Revision Questions

1 What do you understand by the following terms:
hinterland; Central Place; Central Place function; nesting of Central Place functions; nesting of trade areas; k-factor; homogeneous landscape.
2 How do the hinterlands of ports differ from those of service centres in a Central Place system?
3 Why is a hexagonal arrangement of trade areas more efficient than a circular pattern?
4 List the factors which can distort the geometric arrangement of trade areas as suggested by Christaller.
5 Why are the hexagonal patterns of trade areas more likely to be found in areas with an agricultural background?
6 Outline three different methods of measuring spheres of influence.
7 Which methods of delimiting spheres of influence are the (a) most (b) least effective? Explain your answer.
8 What do you understand by the terms: (a) Range of Good (b) Threshold Population?
9 Outline a method of assessing the threshold of a Central Place good.
10 What are the chief problems involved in measuring thresholds?
11 Can the ideas suggested by Christaller relating to spheres of influence be put to use in a practical way? If so, outline some of the ways this has happened.
12 Describe the relationship between Central Places and the size of their trade areas. How can this relationship be shown graphically?

CHAPTER FOUR
SETTLEMENT STRUCTURE

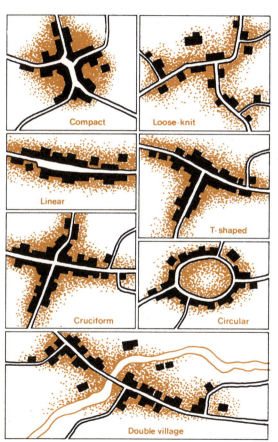

Fig. 4:1 Village shapes: (a) compact; (b) loose-knit; (c) linear;
(d) T-shaped; (e) cruciform; (f) double; (g) circular.

In this chapter we shall cover a number of aspects of the form, shape and structure of buildings and land uses in settlements. These features can be identified in all settlements although a variety of patterns can occur. If we take the shape of villages as an illustration, a possible classification might recognize seven types: compact, loose-knit, linear, T-shaped, cruciform, circular and double. These types are shown in Fig. 4:1 and the characteristics of the different types are discussed in Chapter 6. The different patterns result from the interplay of the factors of local relief, transport routes, economic function and historical evolution of land ownership and settlement form and function. Many villages are the products of natural growth. This means that the form has evolved without direct attempts at organization of the plan of streets and buildings. By contrast we can recognize a group known as planned villages (Fig. 4:2). These are the result of deliberate decisions about function and form. In fact this simple division into two types is slightly artificial. In many villages which resulted from natural growth, the direction and rate of development were dictated by powerful landowners such as the Lord of the Manor or the Church. Similarly, transport routes exercise considerable influence upon the shape of many villages, moulding the pattern into a particular form.

These factors also affect the shape of towns and cities. There are examples of regularly-shaped urban settlements such as the rectangular or grid plans of many American towns. Other common tendencies include circular and stellar (star-shaped) forms but most urban centres have complex elongated, tentacular shapes because of the

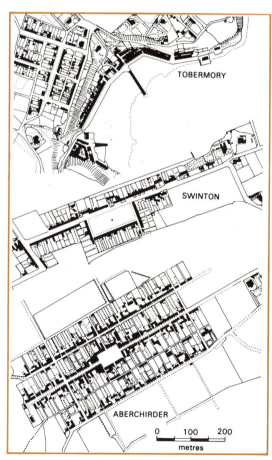

Fig. 4:2 Form of planned villages. Tobermory, 1879, grid modified by relief and coastline. Swinton, 1859, linear with central square. Aberchirder, 1866, grid (D. G. LOCKHART, redrawn from first edition O.S. plans).

Fig. 4:3 Buildings in the Cotswolds: (a) Bibury; (b) Arlington Row, Bibury; (c) Tetbury; (d) Lower Slaughter.

influences of relief and transport upon the directions of growth.

Morphology

This term refers to the pattern of streets, plots and buildings. These can be examined within any settlement and between settlements to investigate similarities and differences. For example, different building materials and styles are a means of inter-settlement comparisons, the comparison of different settlements. Distinct regional types occur such as the cottages and houses at Bibury, Tetbury and Lower Slaughter which are built with the mellow local Cotswold stone (Figs. 4:3a-d). Equally distinctive regional types include the half-timbered buildings of Herefordshire with their famous black and white colouring, e.g. the village of Weobley. Another regional group are the slate-roofed stone cottages of the Lake District.

Traditional building forms include the Scottish tenement which houses from eight to twenty-four families in one block. A refurbished tenement is shown in Fig. 4:4. In this example, the common stairway links four floors and the boundaries of the block are marked by the external drain pipes. Other examples of regional building forms include the brick-built terraces of the mill towns of Northern England and the mining villages of South Wales.

Townscapes

Groups of similar buildings create distinctive elements of the settlement landscape known as townscapes. Apart from their characteristic appearance in terms of building materials and style they are also identified in terms of the spacing of the buildings, the arrangement of the build-

Fig. 4:4 A refurbished tenement, Dalry district of Edinburgh.

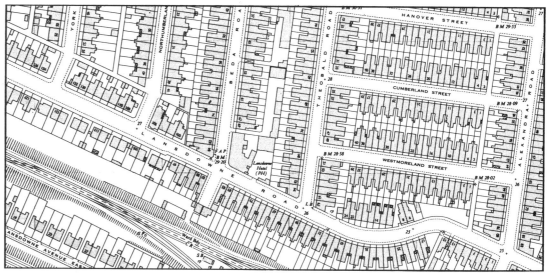

Fig. 4:5 Townscape of 19th century terraced housing, Cardiff.

Fig. 4:6 Townscape of 19th century stone tenements, Glasgow.

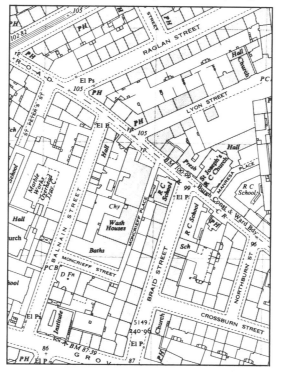

ing plots, the pattern of streets and the land use of the area. Townscapes can be recognized in the field and also from Ordnance Survey maps. Figs. 4:5-4:8 illustrate four distinct townscapes. In the case of areas of nineteenth-century working-class brick-built terraces (Fig. 4:5) and stone-built tenements (Fig. 4:6), there is a marked regularity and linearity to the pattern. The tightly-packed design gives an impression of a densely-peopled area with a very restricted amount of green space (gardens, parks, etc.). There is often a number of industrial firms and warehouses set within the housing. Roads, railways and canals may also be present adding to the congestion and detracting from the environmental attractiveness of these areas. The large local population requires various facilities such as shops, schools and churches and these functions must seek appropriate sites. Shops may be attracted to a corner site which offers accessibility to a number of streets. Shops can occupy the ground floor of a terraced house or tenement block but schools and churches need a complete plot and special buildings. As a result schools and churches often fill gaps in the pattern of housing in these areas unless they acquired a site at an early stage in the development of the area. Although these areas were built before the introduction of modern planning rules, they do show a measure of regularity in design which

suggests that they were not built in a completely haphazard fashion. Some were carefully designed but more often the layout reflects the fact that developers bought pieces of land (fields) and then had to fit their buildings into the shape of that piece of land. These portions of land varied in size (a few houses to many streets) and shape. An irregular shape often resulted in odd corner blocks when the developer tried to use all of the land right up to the boundary (Fig. 4:9). Large pieces of land tend to result in substantial sections of a particular townscape.

Two modern lower density housing areas are shown in Figs. 4:7 and 4:8. One (4:7) illustrates a peripheral local authority owned housing area. There are still strong linear and block-like features in the plan but there are noticeable differences when compared with Figs. 4:5 and 4:6. There is more green space in the modern design and the layout of buildings is more fragmented. Few non-residential land uses are present. An attempt has been made to separate vehicles from play areas. Shops are clustered into a small group often located centrally within the housing area and schools and churches are more widely spaced

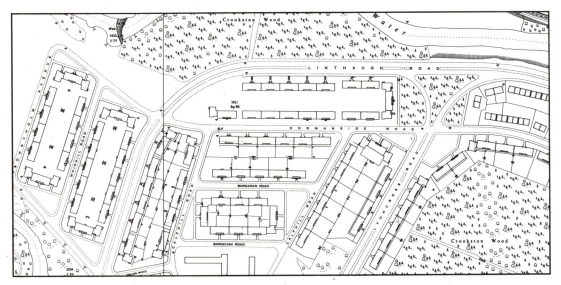

Fig. 4:7 *Townscape of post 1945 local authority estate, Glasgow.*

Fig. 4:8 *Townscape of Victorian villas, Glasgow.*

Fig. 4:9 *Strangely-shaped plots reflect attempts to make full use of the available land.*

Fig. 4:10 Townscape of a housing area in East Kilbride New Town.

than in the nineteenth-century areas because of the lower density of population. Industry is normally placed into separate locations on industrial estates. In general the environment is more attractively planned. The types of houses depend upon a number of factors such as date of development, demand for housing and the housing policies of the local authority. The main types are semi-detached, terraces, and various blocks ranging from four to over thirty storeys.

Although Fig. 4:8 also illustrates a modern housing environment, this example shows an affluent owner-occupied district of semi-detached and detached gardened properties. The sweeping curves of the streets emphasize the desire for privacy and seclusion and the marked pattern of plot boundaries reveals the importance of establishing the exact extent of each piece of land. Such districts are almost entirely residential with shops and schools located on the margins of the area, especially beside the main access routes. Planners have attempted to create aspects of these environments in New Towns (Fig. 4:10) and in new local authority residential areas (Fig. 4:11).

Assignment

1 Make a list of **(a)** the similarities between Figs. 4:8 and 4:10 or 4:11 and **(b)** the differences. Can you suggest reasons for any differences? (You could consider factors such as period of development and ownership of the houses.)

Modern planning has tended to reduce some of the differences in the design and appearance of different types of residential areas. The widespread adoption of particular styles of building and materials has also reduced the degree to which modern townscapes display a distinctive regional flavour. Recently there has been some reaction to this trend and regional styles have

Fig. 4:11 A new residential and industrial development, Tweedbank near Galashiels.

Fig. 4:12a Preservation of old buildings in central Jedburgh.

returned in both new buildings and in the preservation of old properties. Examples of the latter occur in central Jedburgh (4:12a) and Norwich (4:12b). In addition, many old buildings remain in settlements which provide illustrations of earlier regional styles.

These differing trends can be seen at a variety of spatial scales from the local to the international level. The tendency towards an international style is most apparent in new office blocks, hotels, hospitals and airports. By contrast, the local element is especially noticeable in cheap housing which has not been built by local or national government, e.g. shanty towns in Third World cities (Fig. 4:13).

Streets

Once established, the major elements of morphology, the line of streets and the pattern of plots, prove persistent features of the structure of settlements. Plots are the basic unit of property on whch we erect buildings whilst streets are underlain by services such as water, sewerage, electricity, gas and telephones. To alter the line of a street would mean the cost of replacing these services which are placed under streets to allow access for maintenance. Equally, changing the pattern of plots involves negotiating with other owners. Both situations discourage frequent or

Fig. 4:12b Preservation of old buildings in a pedestrianised portion of central Norwich.

Fig. 4:13 Shanty housing, Baroda, India.

dramatic alteration but neither prevent change occurring. In general it is easier to alter the plot arrangement than the pattern of streets, so that the morphology is constantly changing in detail but only experiences an occasional major piece of surgery such as the building of a motorway or the demolition (Fig. 4:14) and reconstruction of a complete area.

Buildings

These are more susceptible to change in both external appearance and internal design. The use may also change and this can cause internal re-organization or complete rebuilding. For example, the conversion of the ground floor of a house into a small shop might only involve the removal of some internal walls and the installation of larger windows to display the goods being sold. Other changes can be more extensive and require the construction of a special building designed to suit the new use. For example, in the 1950s and 1960s many cinemas closed. Where the cinema occupied a prominent site in a major shopping street large shops purchased the property, demolished the old building and constructed new premises to satisfy their requirements for the display, handling and storage of the goods sold in the shop. Sometimes quite a lot of alteration can occur without actually knocking down the existing building.

The conversion of a large terraced house into offices may involve internal work, including new toilets and even the installation of a lift, and external changes, such as the conversion of the rear garden into a car park, but the walls and roof of the old houses may remain as they were.

An interesting example of conversion is an old mill at Bourton-on-the-Water in the Cotswolds

Fig. 4:14 Redevelopment can cause morphological change. An area of 19th century tenements in Glasgow has been cleared in preparation for the construction of the new Springburn Shopping Centre which opened in November 1981.

Fig. 4:15 Old mill at Bourton-on-the-Water which is now used as a transport museum.

Fig. 4:16 A building society office in an old Cotswold stone building in Tetbury.

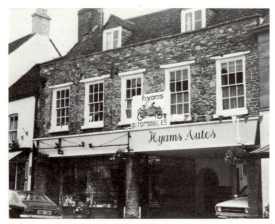

Fig. 4:17 New buildings can use old stone in an attempt to merge with surrounding older buildings, as in this example from Malmesbury.

(Fig. 4:15) which is now used as a motor museum. Planners can exert an influence and require that the new owners maintain the character of the building (Fig. 4:16 and 4:17).

The life of a building varies from a few decades to many centuries. It can be prolonged by regular restoration as in the case of castles, palaces and churches. Fig. 4:18 shows the site of the Roman baths at Bath surrounded by later Georgian buildings where fashionable people once 'took the waters' and listened to orchestras whilst having afternoon tea. Like many historic buildings this site is now a tourist attraction which increases the likelihood that it will be preserved. Ruined buildings are also preserved although expense may not justify restoration (Fig. 4:19). At the other extreme, a very short life normally results from neglect, war or change of function.

Assignment

2 Make a list of buildings in your local town or district which are more than 100 years old. You could list them in groups on the basis of **(a)** architectural style **(b)** materials **(c)** function. Are there any relationships between the different lists?

Plots

Building plots are normally rectangular. The narrow portion is the street frontage with the longer section stretching behind the street frontage. We can see the pattern of plots from an examination of the front of a line of buildings (Fig. 4:20).

In many British settlements past growth resulted in the building of additional properties in the gardens of the original house plots (Fig. 4:21). Sometimes this led to serious housing and medical problems in periods before the introduction of domestic sewerage facilities and the development of modern medical knowledge. One response was to clear these areas in order to reduce population densities and produce a more open morphology. In the 1870s schemes of this type were implemented in parts of the central areas of many British cities, e.g. London, Birmingham, Glasgow and Edinburgh. In Birmingham some of these new streets became in

Fig. 4:18 Roman baths and Georgian pump room, Bath.

Fig. 4:19 Jedburgh Abbey.

Fig. 4:20 Plot divisions can be identified from the major vertical lines of the fronts of the buildings.

Fig. 4:21 Overbuilding on the rear of plots, once garden space, behind High Street, Hawick.

time major shopping streets, e.g. Corporation Street. Elsewhere the new streets were minor features. In Glasgow a substantial area of poor housing, near the eastern edge of the centre at Gallowgate, was cleared during the construction of a railway leading to St. Enoch Station.

Apart from infilling vacant space in plots or redesigning the pattern by such clearance schemes, the pattern can be changed in other ways. Adjacent plots may be bought and amalgamated to give a larger property. This action may be essential when a change of function is planned such as the building of a large shop on sites previously occupied by two houses. On occasion only parts, either the front or rear portions, of the original plots may be altered. For example, the rear portions may be collected to give a new substantial plot for a clinic or offices or a car park. Equally, the front portions may be gathered together to provide sufficient space for a shopping centre or a hotel. You can gain an insight into the pattern by examining aerial photographs and large-scale maps of the central area of a settlement. Fig. 4:22 shows the morphology of the central area of York. Notice the influence of the Minster on the layout of the surrounding area. There was also a town wall which bounded the medieval area. Features such as churches, castles and town walls exercised an influence upon the morphology. The wall limited the extent of the urban area and, if population growth occurred, encouraged the infilling of vacant spaces within the walls. As a result these areas often have a dense pattern of development.

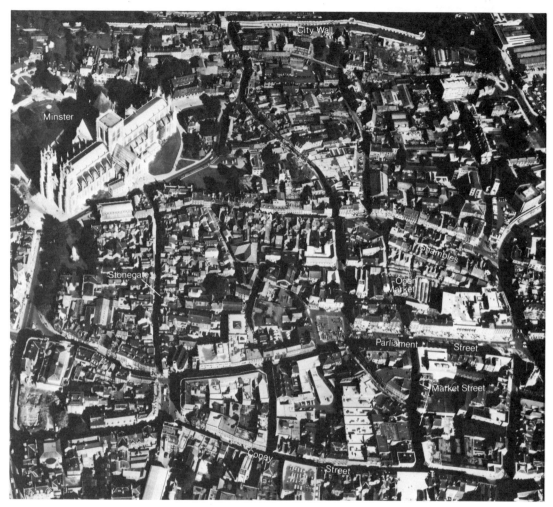

Fig. 4:22 The morphology of central York.

This can be seen in the vicinity of Stonegate. Churches or castles acted as obstacles or barriers to development, in addition to influencing the type of buildings in the adjoining area. In York a considerable area of church property is still located beside the Minster.

In Fig. 4:22 there is a marked contrast between the tightly-packed buildings beside Stonegate and the comparatively open pattern in the Market Street-Parliament Street area. The density of development does not necessarily measure the economic importance of the two areas. Stonegate contains book shops and other craft and specialist shops whereas the main variety stores and department stores are situated in Parliament Street and Coney Street.

There is often a difference in the morophology on opposite sides of a wall. This boundary can outlast the actual feature as in Vienna where the wall was demolished and a ring road built in its place but the road still separates old medieval Vienna from the more regular streets of the nineteenth-century city.

Assignment
3   Study Fig. 4:22 and write notes on
    (a)   the street pattern, and
    (b)   the plot pattern.

Functional Zones

When we examine a large city such as Sheffield (Fig. 4:23) the first impression is one of the complex arrangement of land uses. However, careful examination suggests that there are various zones of industry, offices and shops, housing and green space. In other words, order does exist. Some functional zones are devoted to one function, e.g. expensive houses. Other zones involve a number of associated land uses. An example of that situation is the Central Business District (C.B.D.) which mainly contains shops and offices but includes other functions such as railway and bus stations, some industries, warehouses and various public buildings (e.g. the post office, town hall).

How can we explain the arrangement of zones? First, some functions require special sites, e.g. flat land. Second, and more commonly, some need certain situations. For example, shops must be accessible if they are to survive by attracting customers. Third, different functions can be attracted by the qualities of a particular site. This competition must be resolved and if zones are to result, similar land uses occupy the site and different uses seek other locations. Fourth, not all land uses face the same pressures to get a particular site. Hence, there are differences in intensity of competition. Finally, it may not be possible to obtain the desired location because of cost, unwillingness of the owner to sell, or opposition from planners or other pressure groups.

It may not be possible to find functional zones in small settlements. We might expect the shops to be located near the centre of the village but on occasion they can be situated near the edge. In this situation, the complicating factors are

Fig. 4:23 Sheffield.

dominant. For example, village shops are often situated in part of the owner's house. The choice of location therefore involves the site of the owner's house as well as the shop. In any case, the small distances involved in the village situation may mean that there is not a major difference for the customer between a central and less central location. This is especially relevant when the shop also serves surrounding farms and hamlets.

In towns and cities, the pattern in some areas can be complicated because of remnants from preceding periods. Normally functional zones can be identified in the field and from photographs or maps. Two bundles of factors are especially important in shaping the pattern of functional zones: economic considerations and planning policies. Planning is dominant in communist countries, e.g. Russia, whereas, in Britain, the pattern is the outcome of economic considerations and planning policies. We shall examine the planning of New Towns in Britain in Chapter 5. In older settlements British planners have concentrated upon the reshaping and improvement of the existing structure.

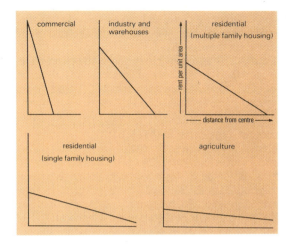

Fig. 4:24 The rent curves of major types of land use (B. BERRY).

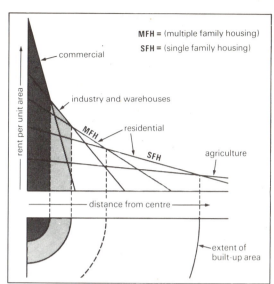

Fig. 4:25 The land use pattern created by allocating space on the basis of the highest bid rent (G. J. FIELDING).

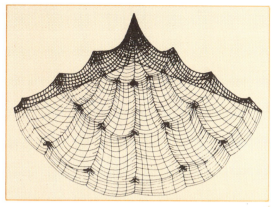

Fig. 4:27 Land value surface which includes minor nodes of accessibility such as suburban shopping centres (after J. SIMMONS).

Economic influences offer an explanation of land use patterns when sites are sold to the highest bidder. A site at the heart of the city at the hub of transport routes is very attractive for major shops because it gives the best opportunity to attract the largest number of customers. The cost of such sites is very high because there is a very limited supply. Within a few hundred metres you have moved away from the concentration of transport routes and much of the quality of accessibility to many customers is lost. A shop would pay much less for sites in these streets. This argument can be applied to any type of land use. Certain sites are particularly attractive for housing because of the view or the area or the situation in relation to other parts of the city. People will pay more for houses in attractive situations than in unpleasant positions. For each land use a graph can be drawn showing the amount of rent in relation to distance from the centre of the city (Fig. 4:24). In general the lines, known as bid-rent curves, slope downwards as we move away from the city centre, illustrating the economic importance of accessibility. However, the slope differs between various land uses. If we place all the lines on one graph (Fig. 4:25) it becomes apparent that at specific locations if the site goes to the highest bidder a particular type of land use will dominate.

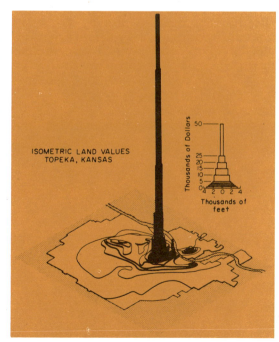

Fig. 4:26 The land value surface of Topeka, Kansas (D. KNOS).

In this case the centre will consist of a zone of shops and offices, then industry and warehouses, followed by housing and finally, agriculture. A concentric series of functional zones would result.

Urban areas have a topography of land values (Fig. 4:26) with a peak at the centre and much smaller peaks at other places with an above average level of accessibility, e.g. suburban shopping centres. The simple pattern shown in Fig. 4:25 is complicated by these lesser centres to produce the situation illustrated by Fig. 4:27.

Why should we expect land values to decline as we move away from the centre? The explanation relates to the amount of land or sites. At the centre it is very restricted but there are many points one kilometre from the centre and many more at five kilometres. In other words, the supply varies. So does demand. Central sites are few in number in relation to demand and therefore expensive. Sometimes demand can cause the price of other locations to rise. For example, if urban extension is restricted by a Green Belt, a zone at the edge of the city in which urban developments are prohibited, then the value of any remaining empty site will probably rise.

Other criteria such as age of buildings and population density also produce concentric zones.

Inner residential areas have higher densities than outer suburbs and the age of building tends to decline as we move outward from the centre. A simple model would have three zones: the C.B.D., the inner high density residential zone; the outer suburbs. Redevelopment is altering this pattern because in demolishing and rebuilding the inner areas of cities, the population density is reduced and new buildings replace old properties.

Models of Urban Structure

E. W. Burgess, an American sociologist, proposed the concentric model of urban structure shown in Fig. 4:28. Burgess argued that competition between different land uses resulted in an orderly pattern of zones. The model was a generalization from a study of Chicago (Fig. 4:29). Of course, many factors complicate the pattern in reality. Thus the eastern portion of the circles in the case of Chicago were absent because of Lake Michigan.

Burgess simplifies the situation by assuming a flat area with equal accessibility in all directions and a logical method of competition for sites, e.g. rent-paying ability. Change started at the centre and spread outwards through the zones. Shops

and offices would invade the next zone and when they became dominant the stage of succession was reached. In the same way other zones could extend outward.

The importance of planning, changes in accessibility in cities and the role of local authority housing are all major additional features in British cities which are not present in the Burgess model. It could also be argued that attitudes about the way sites should be allocated can differ from the situation which is assumed in the model. Of course, it would be difficult to construct an international model which would allow economic considerations to be dominant in some situations and religious or planning factors to be decisive in others.

Two other simple patterns have been suggested: sectors and multiple-nuclei.

In a study of American cities, H. Hoyt found that the structure resembled sectors rather than concentric circles. In outlining the sector model (Fig. 4:30) Hoyt stressed the important role of high value housing districts in shaping the overall structure. It was recognized that topography can affect the pattern with high value housing seeking attractive locations. The notion that a particular

type of housing could extend to the edge of the settlement appears to be closer to the real situation than the idea that the outer zone consisted of middle-class housing. However, if the outer zone is described as an area of modern low density housing the concentric concept could also approximate to the general structure of many cities.

Another suggestion is that settlements consist of various focal points or nuclei (Fig. 4:31). The multiple nuclei model does not stress the role of the C.B.D. or of high value housing as major influential zones. Instead a wide range of factors are recognized which encouraged the production of a pattern of functional areas. Harris and Ullman suggested that special site requirements, rent-paying ability, attraction of similar land uses, repulsion of opposed land uses and various other factors (which could include planning or religious attitudes) would all be involved in creating the pattern. In this model the settlement consists of various nuclei which attract particular land uses or associations of land uses.

A composite model (Fig. 4:32) has been developed by P. H. Mann. This includes con-

Fig. 4:28 *The concentric model of urban structure (E. BURGESS).*

Fig. 4:29 *Urban zones in Chicago in the 1920s (E. BURGESS).*

Fig. 4:30 *Sector model of urban structure (H. HOYT).*

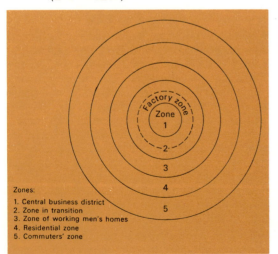

Zones:
1. Central business district
2. Zone in transition
3. Zone of working men's homes
4. Residential zone
5. Commuters' zone

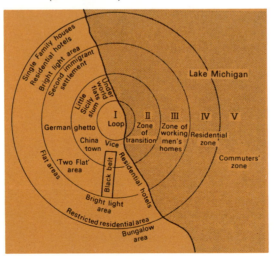

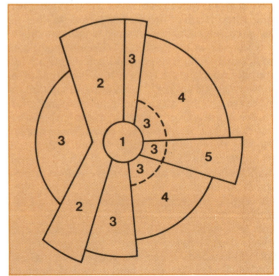

centric zones and sectors. In addition he further shaped the pattern by introducing the influence of the direction of the prevailing wind. Mann argued that high value housing would seek locations away from the outfall zones of wind-borne pollution. The model is useful in the British context but it is doubtful if it is any more appropriate than the concentric, sector or multi-nuclei models as a generalization of the structure of cities such as Calcutta or Tehran.

Despite these reservations models are a valuable aid in the analysis of structure because they describe the pattern which should occur under specific conditions. Although these conditions may be complicated by many factors the model can assist our attempts to understand and explain the structure of settlements.

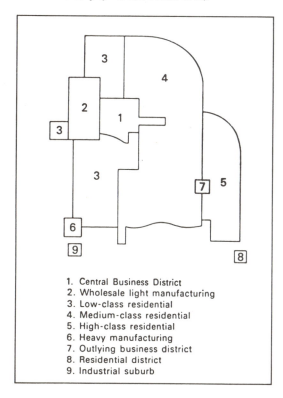

Fig. 4:31 Multiple nuclei model of urban structure (C. HARRIS and E. ULLMAN published in Annals American Academy of Political Science 1945).

1. Central Business District
2. Wholesale light manufacturing
3. Low-class residential
4. Medium-class residential
5. High-class residential
6. Heavy manufacturing
7. Outlying business district
8. Residential district
9. Industrial suburb

There is a general relationship between the size of settlement and the intensity of land use competition. We would expect competition to be greater at the centre of a large city than a small town. Indeed in a small settlement the pattern of functional zones may be blurred. Because rents are

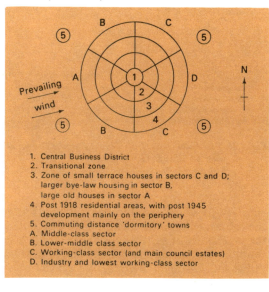

Fig. 4:32 The structure of the British industrial city (P. MANN).

1. Central Business District
2. Transitional zone
3. Zone of small terrace houses in sectors C and D; larger bye-law housing in sector B, large old houses in sector A
4. Post 1918 residential areas, with post 1945 development mainly on the periphery
5. Commuting distance 'dormitory' towns
A. Middle-class sector
B. Lower-middle class sector
C. Working-class sector (and main council estates)
D. Industry and lowest working-class sector

Fig. 4:33 A farm situated within 80 metres of the main road and less than 250 metres from the centre of Malmesbury.

comparatively lower, a number of different types of land use may be able to afford central sites. On occasion farms can even be located quite close to the centre (Fig. 4:33).

Assignment

4 Examine Figs. 4:34 and 4:35 which show models of the structure of cities in South-East Asia and Eastern Europe. Compare these models with the concentric model. Make a list of (a) similarities (b) differences. Could any of the differences be explained by differences in political organization?

The Central Business District (C.B.D.)

This area has traditionally been the centre of the transport network, a fact which gives considerable centrality to locations in the C.B.D. As a result certain activities are attracted to the area. The principal characteristics of the C.B.D. are:

1. It is the focal point of the transport system
2. There is a concentration of department stores, variety stores and specialist shops
3. There are distinct clusters of administrative, commercial and professional offices
4. Competition for sites will encourage multi-storey developments giving a vertical component to the area

Fig. 4:34 Model of the structure of a socialist city (A. DAWSON).

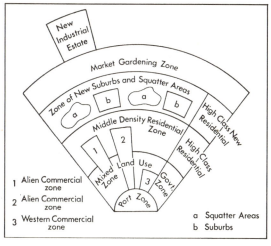

1 Alien Commercial zone
2 Alien Commercial zone
3 Western Commercial zone
a Squatter Areas
b Suburbs

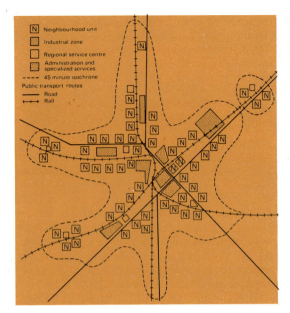

Fig. 4:35 *Generalised structure of a large South-east Asian City (T. McGEE).*

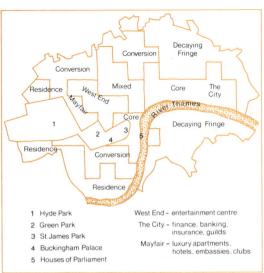

1 Hyde Park
2 Green Park
3 St. James Park
4 Buckingham Palace
5 Houses of Parliament

West End – entertainment centre
The City – finance, banking, insurance, guilds
Mayfair – luxury apartments, hotels, embassies, clubs

Fig. 4:36 *Functional zones of the Central Business District of London (after J. GODDARD).*

Fig. 4:37 *The Corridor, Bath, an example of an enclosed shopping lane or arcade linking two shopping streets.*

Fig. 4:38 *The Corridor, Bath.*

5. The core is surrounded by transport termini and car parks
6. Some industries are present such as fashion clothing and newspaper publication but they are situated away from the principal shopping streets
7. Few houses exist apart from the flats of caretakers and small clusters of high cost housing (Mayfair, London)
8. There is a distinct population geography with a vast daytime population but few people at night
9. A number of functional zones occur which relate to factors such as land values and accessibility (Fig. 4:36).

The C.B.D. does change. Rebuilding is commonplace reflecting changes in tastes, demand, use and opportunities. Through time the area can migrate by invading new areas and abandoning earlier sites. In London, for example, the principal direction of growth was westward although recently development has occurred at riverside sites and locations near the Bank of England at the eastern edge of the C.B.D. This may reflect the availability of suitable sites but it could also result from planning controls seeking to prevent the abandonment of parts of the central area. Notable examples of this type of site are the old fruit market locations in many British cities, e.g. Covent Garden, London. A further example of a substantial site undergoing redevelopment is the St. Enoch Station area in Glasgow which has been cleared and plans have been approved for an office development.

In general the C.B.D. is an area of keen competition for sites and comparatively high values but considerable variation occurs within the zone. Intense competition is largely restricted to the prime sites on the main shopping streets. This situation can lead to attempts to extend the shopping area through the building of arcades or malls (Fig. 4:37). The Corridor in Bath (Fig. 4:38) is, in effect, an enclosed alley between two shopping streets producing the additional shop frontages which are so desirable for display goods such as jewellery.

In Western cities the core of the C.B.D. (shops and offices) is surrounded by a frame of more varied land uses (Fig. 4:39). This frame of less intensive development fades into the zone of transition of the concentric model.

Shops are also found outside the C.B.D. They occur in groups or individually and serve local and district demands.

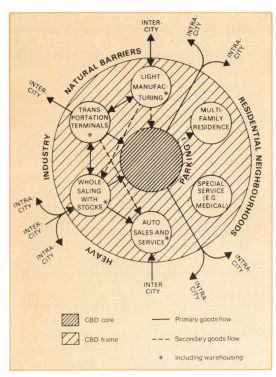

Fig. 4:39 The core and frame of the C.B.D. (HORWOOD and BOYCE).

Recently the dominance of the C.B.D. has been challenged by the growth of large suburban shopping centres and the building of superstores, hypermarkets and discount stores. These new stores carry a wide range of goods apart from foodstuffs. They are situated in locations which seek to benefit from the growth of suburbs and the building of new motorways at the edge of cities. Offices, industry and warehouses have also been attracted to the edge of the city for similar reasons. In addition, these sites are cheaper per square metre than more central locations within the city.

In some American cities these trends have affected the C.B.D., greatly reducing its importance as the major shopping district. Large out-of-town shopping centres with vast parking lots are commonplace features of the suburban areas around American cities. These developments are taking place in Britain but, to date, at a slower rate than in America. British planners have opposed sprawling low-density suburban growth. They have channelled growth into new settlements and redeveloped older, inner areas of cities. Both measures give some encouragement to central shopping districts. Improvements to the transport system in cities and the provision of central parking facilities also support the role of the C.B.D. Nonetheless, major suburban centres, such as Brent Cross in North London, are being developed and there already exists an extensive ring of superstores and discount warehouses around the edge of most British cities. The future importance of the C.B.D. depends upon the relative growth of these new developments compared to the rate of population growth in the settlements.

Assignment

5 What type of C.B.D. functions do you think would suffer from the building of superstores and discount warehouses? Give reasons for your choice. You should consider factors such as accessibility and threshold populations in making your decisions.

Location of Industry

Fig. 4:40 illustrates a possible model of the industrial structure of a metropolis such as London or New York. Four types of locations are identified: central, port, radial and suburban. Central and port locations have been discussed previously. Industries at central sites place a premium on accessibility whilst port industries are attracted by the availability of raw materials at the port. Radial and suburban locations share common characteristics such as access to modern transport routes, mainly roads, and the availability of fairly large sites at lower cost than more central locations.

At one time unpleasant or smelly industries were often banished to suburban locations but modern industries do not normally present these problems.

Industrial estates have been built in suburban locations because of the availability of land and

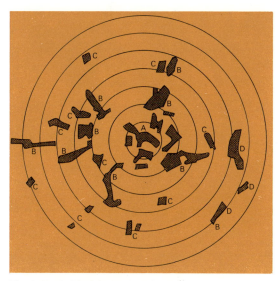

Fig. 4:40 Model of the location of industry in a city (F. HAMILTON).

the general compatibility of light industry, which produces little pollution, and residential environments. In any case the estates are separated by grassland from the housing areas. Estates such as Trafford Park in Manchester date from the nineteenth century but modern estates of light industry and warehouses were started in the 1930s in a direct attempt to produce new jobs in urban settlements for industrial workers. The buildings on the estate are laid out in a regular design. They are often built by the authority operating the estate and then rented to industrialists. Transport routes link the estate to the remainder of the urban area although many minor roads within the estate are narrow and not designed to carry heavy loads or dense flows of vehicles.

We could add two further locations to the model. First, locations related to past periods such as canal or riverside sites. Some industries may remain on these sites although the original attractions are now irrelevant, e.g. sawmills beside canals. Second, a group which might be described as random in location. Single factories set in residential areas. Often they can be explained by

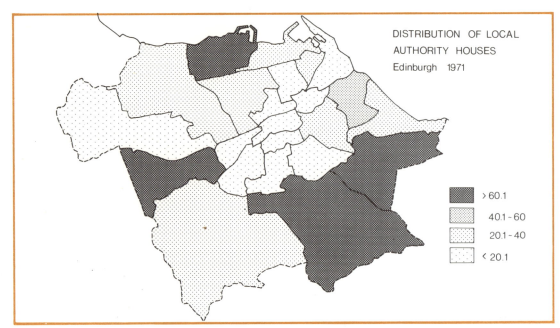

DISTRIBUTION OF LOCAL AUTHORITY HOUSES

Edinburgh 1971

> 60.1

40.1 - 60

20.1 - 40

< 20.1

Fig. 4:41 Distribution of local authority houses, Edinburgh, 1971.

Fig. 4:42 Distribution of private rented houses, Edinburgh, 1971.

DISTRIBUTION OF PRIVATE RENTED HOUSES
EDINBURGH 1971

> 50.1

25.1 - 50

10.1 - 25

< 10

0   3km

considering the site when the factory was built. Such factories probably acquired sites at the edge of settlements or in partly developed districts but subsequent urban growth has left them isolated within residential districts.

Residential Areas

Residential land use accounts for about half of the urban area of large settlements and a much larger share of small places.

Many features can be used to identify different types of residential areas. These can be separated into two broad groups. First, studies which use features of buildings such as age, materials, facilities and type of ownership. Second, those based upon the characteristics of households such as occupation, education, religion and ethnic origin. The second group is often described by the term the social patterning of settlements.

Housing is a major topic of Chapter 5 so only a few examples will be examined here as illustrations of these two approaches.

There are three main forms of housing tenure in Britain; owner-occupation, renting from the local authority and renting from private landlords. During this century the proportion of houses occupied by their owners or rented from a local authority have increased but the share of the total number of houses accounted for by those rented from private landlords has fallen sharply.

At one time most working-class families lived in houses which were rented from private landlords. By 1918 construction of these properties had virtually ceased largely because rising costs meant that it was no longer an attractive speculation. Local authorities were authorized to build houses to satisfy the needs of these families. As a result the number of local authority houses has grown continuously since 1918, especially in the post-1945 period. These new houses were mostly built at the edge of settlements because of the availability of land. We could therefore expect some sort of spatial pattern of different forms of house tenure to be shown on a map of a city. Notice the predominantly peripheral location of most local authority housing in Fig. 4:41. The contrast with the pattern for private rented properties (Fig.

4:42) for the same city, Edinburgh, is very obvious. Because building almost stopped in 1918 the private rented houses are near the heart of the city in the older districts. Indeed many are so old that they have been knocked down and replaced by modern local authority houses. Finally, the pattern of owner-occupied housing (Fig. 4:43) also reveals distinct concentrations at particular locations. Remember these are not all high value houses. People buy quite small flats in tenements or other small properties in old buildings. There is, therefore, a range of values which cannot be identified merely by mapping the number of owner-occupied houses. We would have to add a measure of house price to distinguish different types of area within this category.

Much information about households can be found in the national decennial Census. The most recent in Britain was conducted in April 1981. Families complete a questionnaire. The questions refer to features such as the size of the family, ages, sex, occupation, type of house and facilities in the house. No one can obtain information about individual families. It is completely confidential. Results are published for groups ranging from areas called enumeration districts (about 200 households) to local government areas such as wards, districts and regions. We can then look for relationships between different features, such as occupation and house type, within areas and make comparisons between areas. Fig. 4:44 shows an example of the maps which can be produced from this sort of study. It is also possible to compare the present pattern with an earlier pattern. This is obviously useful when we may be trying to solve some sort of problem since it provides a measure of change, and to some extent, of success.

Rural-Urban Fringe

There is a sort of frontier zone around urban settlements between the built-up urban area and the rural countryside. This frontier zone will contain some urban land uses set amidst farmland and open space. In part the situation is the inevitable outcome of the pressures for the expansion of the urban area. In addition some urban land uses will be especially attracted to this zone

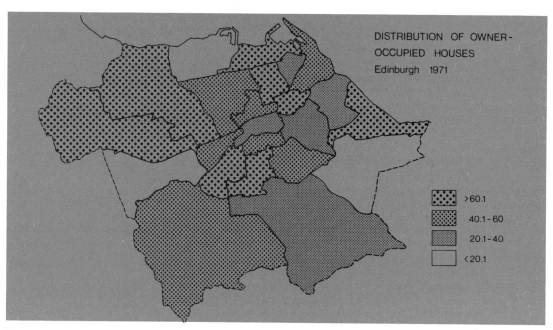

Fig. 4:43 Distribution of owner-occupied houses, Edinburgh, 1971.

Fig. 4:44 Households sharing or lacking a WC, Edinburgh, 1971.

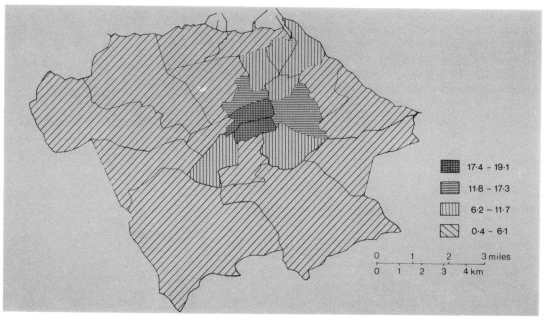

because of the availability of space. Parks, playing fields, and golf courses are all examples of this situation. Less attractive examples are scrapyards and rubbish tips but both occur in the rural-urban fringe. Some people refer to this area as a second zone of transition. This implies that it is changing from rural to urban use. That is often correct but the rate of change can vary greatly and many of these fringe forms of land use, such as golf courses, can remain in existence for many years after the frontier has moved further outward. In fact, we can often identify previous fringe zones by the presence of these land uses. Space consuming uses such as golf courses or hospitals probably acquired fringe locations during a period of slow growth and reduced competition for sites. We can justify this view by pointing to the fact that housing would produce more income for the owner of the site. Hence these large consumers of space may indicate periods of reduced urban expansion in terms of new house-building. Since 1945 planning has influenced the nature and rate of growth and the decisions concerning the use of particular sites. Thus our earlier remarks relate primarily to the nineteenth and early twentieth centuries. Yet the fringe still remains the likely location of any new use which requires a large amount of land at a comparatively low cost, e.g. a motorway interchange or a regional park.

Another aspect of this topic is the movement of families from cities and towns into villages and housing developments set within the rural-urban fringe. This feature is discussed in Chapter 6.

Assignments

6 Survey an area of rural-urban fringe of approximately 4 square kilometres. Compile a land use map. List the urban uses and attempt an explanation of their locations. You should define the urban edge of the area by the boundary of the continuously built-up area but this may need to be adjusted to suit particular situations. The area should include an 'A' class road. (It is possible to base this exercise on aerial photographs and maps although it is preferable to include some fieldwork.)

7 Look at Fig. 4:45 and draw a simple plan of the morphology of Cirencester. Write brief notes on the main areas shown on your plan.

8 Examine Fig. 4:46 and write short notes on this townscape.

9 Cover Fig. 4:47 with a sheet of tracing paper and plot the pattern of bottle-shaped kilns. Using a different symbol mark other industries on your tracing. Write notes on the distribution of housing in Fig. 4:47. You should refer to the relationship to other land uses such as industry, shops, transport routes and open space.

10 Fig. 4:48 shows a suburban shopping centre in Moscow. Study a suburban centre in your district and list the principal features of each centre.

Revision Questions

1 List the chief factors which affect the form of villages under the separate headings: Physical Factors; Human Factors. For each factor listed write a brief note on its particular effect.

2 What do you understand by the following terms: Morphology; Townscapes; Linear pattern of streets; Low density housing; Regional style of housing?

3 Describe the various types of change which can occur in settlements in relation to: Street patterns; Types and style of buildings; Function of buildings.

4 How did changes in the density of population and density of buildings affect the morphology of towns? Give some examples to illustrate your answer.

5 What are Functional Zones? List and describe the different types of functional zones found within a large urban area.

6 Which are the most important factors influencing the emergence of different functional zones in a city? Briefly explain the effect of each factor listed.

7 What are bid-rent curves? Briefly describe the changing pattern of rents as you move from the city centre to the edge of the city.

8 Why do land values decline as we move away from city centre areas?

9 List the main elements of the concentric circle model.

10 How has town planning affected the structure of urban settlements?

11 What is a Central Business District? Describe the main types of establishments which you would expect to find in this particular area of a city.

12 How is the location of industry in a city affected by the following:
   (a) Space availability
   (b) Accessibility
   (c) Residential areas
   (d) Transport costs.

Fig. 4:45
Cirencester.

Fig. 4:46 Inter-war housing, Southampton.

Fig. 4:47 Potteries industrial landscape. The distinctive bottle-shaped kilns have now been demolished and the area redeveloped.

Fig. 4:48 Suburban shopping centre, Moscow.

CHAPTER FIVE
ISSUES IN URBAN SETTLEMENTS

Introduction

A variety of physical, economic, social, environmental and planning issues occur in most large urban settlements. Physical growth consumes farmland and necessitates the creation of an array of urban services such as houses, transport, schools and hospitals. There is, therefore, competition for land and also for finance to create these services. A major economic problem is the supply of employment opportunities for the urban population. All areas may have general problems of job creation but they are particularly noticeable in urban centres. This is caused by the concentration of people, the process of **agglomeration**, which is so characteristic of urban society. Many people are engaged in the same specialized tasks, be it working in a factory or a shop or an office. The closure of one large firm inevitably leads to a corresponding increase in unemployment unless new jobs become available. The latter requires either economic growth or that other firms wanted more workers but were unable to find people to fill these vacancies. In periods of slow economic growth demand for additional workers is low and therefore redundancy is likely to lead to short-term, and possibly long-term (more than one year), unemployment.

Urban settlements also face a series of social and environmental problems. For example, there may be a problem relating to the quality of housing or to the total supply of housing. Most British industrial towns and cities have been grappling with the problem of the quality of housing for much of the twentieth century. In the last few decades many cities in Third World countries have experienced massive population growth which has generated a corresponding demand for housing. One result has been the development of the squatter settlements which have become a characteristic feature of almost all cities in these countries (Fig. 4:13). These settlements vary in location (central or peripheral), size (hundreds to thousands of houses), and permanency but they are a major source of minimal standard, often unplanned, urban housing. Other social problems include levels of crime and vandalism in cities, health problems and problems relating to conflict between groups of different ethnic origin (race or colour) or religious persuasion. Equally, social problems may refer to concentrations of groups which have particular needs. For example, the development of sheltered housing in Britain is an attempt by planners and local authorities to create a residential environment especially designed for elderly people.

There are important links between various problems. Commuting by car creates circulation problems in terms of access to cities (Fig. 5:1) and also movement within cities (Fig. 5:2). In addition, pollution from car exhausts can cause a health hazard in that lead levels in the blood of people living near urban motorways may be dangerously high. It certainly creates atmospheric pollution with significant consequences in fog-prone environments such as Los Angeles.

Urban or industrial decay can also cause environmental problems at a variety of scales ranging from a local eyesore in a housing area to the despoliation of the environment of a region by industrial or mineral waste. Where the materials are poisonous, the area may have to be left for many years before it can be used by man for

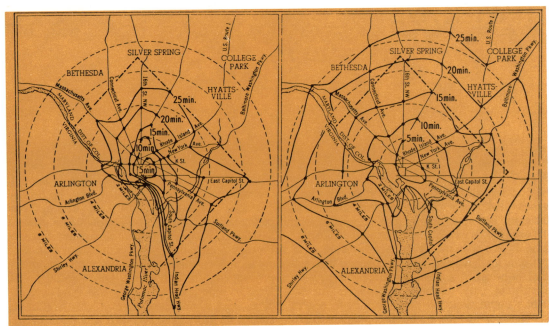

Fig. 5:1 Differences in travel speeds in Washington D.C. at evening rush hour and one hour later. When the volume of traffic is less much greater distances can be travelled in a set amount of time when compared to rush hour conditions.

another activity, e.g. housing or recreation. It may be even longer before the land could be converted to or revert to agricultural use because of the dangers of poisoning through crops or livestock.

Planners seek solutions to these various problems. Green Belts, New Towns, new housing, traffic-management schemes and the reclamation of industrial and mineral workings are all measures which have achieved substantial success. Nonetheless, many problems remain unsolved. This is partly because there is no perfect solution. Agglomeration of population, for example, will almost inevitably lead to some problems of movement. In many developed countries, the problem is associated with the car and the consequent demand for parking-space in towns and cities (Fig. 5:3) and improved roads. In China, there is congestion in cities but it is associated with commuters on bicycles, so there are fewer

problems in terms of parking-space, special roads or atmospheric pollution. A second point is that many problems take some time to solve. There can often be an interval of ten years between the planning and construction stages in development. An additional difficulty is that in the meantime the problem may have changed in intensity or character. It may have become more severe so the original plan becomes inadequate. Alternatively, the problem may have decreased so that the planned development is now unnecessary. Even more frustrating is the situation where it changes in character. There may, for example, still be a demand for housing but not of the type which was originally planned or at that sort of location. Some British authorities have only recently completed the last multi-storey flats which they planned in the 1960s, even though such buildings have become unpopular as a source of general housing, i.e. housing designed

for everyone, young or old, people with families or with no family. This is not meant to imply that everyone dislikes living in multi-storey houses but merely that authorities now consider that they are not suited to particular situations.

Finally, many problems are, to some extent, relative. What we consider to be a problem may not have been seen as a problem fifty years ago, e.g. industrial pollution. The definition of problems also varies between countries. Housing considered completely inadequate in Britain might rate quite highly in developing countries. This is due to factors such as people's expectations, their levels of income, cultural characteristics and planning standards. If we consider an analogy for a moment the situation is readily understood. In English football when Liverpool are not in the leadership race, commentators start to say that the team has problems. Similarly, in Scotland, Celtic and Rangers are expected to dominate the championship and capture most trophies. The expectations of these clubs, therefore, are very high. But they are in a competitive situation and it is impossible, unless there is something wrong with the competition, for them always to be completely successful. Success for another club might mean avoiding relegation or reaching a particular round in a cup competition. When we discuss issues in urban settlements it is worth bearing this analogy in mind. Many countries cannot afford the cost of some solutions. Moreover, when a solution is adopted, the opposition (the problem) may change tactics (increase, decrease, or alter in character) and the team (urban settlement) may still face a crisis in terms of their level of performance (satisfying the critics such as pressure groups or the electorate).

The remainder of the chapter discusses some of these physical, economic, social and environmental issues.

Urban Growth

There are three major points.

1. Competition for land between urban and other land uses such as agriculture
2. An associated feature is the shape and direction of urban growth, introducing questions concerning sprawl and controls

Fig. 5:2 Traffic restrictions in central York.

Fig. 5:3 Car parking in the middle of the main street of a small market town.

3. Problems within the urban area caused by growth, in physical or population size, such as transportation, housing, or quality of the environment.

The last group is so complex and important that it will be discussed in detail later in the chapter.

In 1901 less than five per cent of all land use in England and Wales was directly related to urban development. More than eighty per cent was associated with agricultural use. By 1971 the urban proportion had more than doubled although between 1901 and 1971 the population of Britain increased only forty-five per cent. The explanations of the disproportionate growth of the urban area primarily relate to lower density residential and industrial developments and new land uses which need large amounts of space e.g. airports and motorways. In cities densely-packed residential areas (Fig. 5:4), terraced or tenement, have been demolished and replaced by modern buildings in lower density schemes (Fig. 5:5). Since the beginning of the century additional peripheral housing has tended to be built at comparatively low density, e.g. 12 houses per acre or 4.85 houses per hectare.

Assignment
1 Visit your local library and study maps of your nearest town or city today and early in the twentieth century. Trace the outline of the urban area from each map. Calculate the area. One method is to shade squares on graph paper and compare the totals. If the maps are of different scales you will have to adjust the figures to a common scale, e.g. square kilometres. Compare the increase in area with the change in population for the same period. Comment on any differences. List examples of low density development and any new major land uses, e.g. industrial estates, major roads, airports, parks, playing fields, etc.

Since four out of every five persons in Britain live in towns or cities you might think that urban growth is not really a serious problem, especially when new developments are quite spacious and planned. The problem is that additional land

Fig. 5:4 19th century back-to-back terrace housing in Leeds. This area has now been redeveloped.

Fig. 5:5 High-rise housing, Roehampton, London. Comprehensive redevelopment of the central areas of cities forced many families to move to peripheral estates like Roehampton.

used for urban settlement must be transferred from some other use. Frequently the transfer is from agricultural use. This had led to controversy with some experts opposing urban growth because it endangers our food supply. Others have pointed to the increased agricultural production from a smaller area as evidence that opposition to urban growth should not assume it endangers the food supply. However, the situation is more complex than these statements suggest. There are different qualities of agricultural land. In Britain we recognize four major categories of land capability (A, B, C and D), with type A (the best) being food fertile land capable of growing most crops and type D (the poorest) land of little agricultural value because of soil quality, relief and climate. Most land of type D is only suited to rough grazing. Generally, the better quality land is confined to land at a fairly low altitude (below 350 metres) and with few prob-

lems of slope or drainage. Urban development in Britain is largely confined within the same altitudinal zone, sea-level to 350 metres. Thus the competition is sharper and more serious than it might initially appear. Urban development often encompasses good quality agricultural land (types A and B). We can, of course, channel urban growth towards poorer quality land, and whenever possible planners try to do this. However, this may mean higher building costs caused by site problems such as drainage and involve special measures such as re-inforced foundations for the buildings.

The complexity of the controversy can be illustrated by the fact that, in Britain, we import more than one-third of our total food supplies. To cut that to zero would require a massive increase in output by British agriculture, an increase which might be impossible to achieve without completely stopping the growth of urban areas. Equally

those favouring urban growth can argue that any loss of agricultural land can be met by some combination of increased production, increased imports and substitution, e.g. synthetic foods. There is not a correct answer to this problem in the sense that you have a correct answer to a sum in arithmetic. The answer depends upon policy decisions about the rôle of home-based agriculture versus imports and on the needs of the urban population for adequate space in which to live, rest and work.

Other groups such as conservationists oppose urban growth because it threatens the habitats of wild plants and animals. Conflict arising from these interests particularly surrounds motorway projects and urban-oriented recreation such as the development of ski-ing facilities in what previously was a wilderness area.

The second issue concerns the nature and direction of urban growth. We have already mentioned the need to avoid using good quality agricultural land. It is also desirable to avoid sprawling linear developments and unfinished projects in which only a tiny proportion of a residential project is completed. Urban sprawl became evident in the 1930s with houses being built alongside main roads but much of the space away from transport routes was left undeveloped. Fig. 5:6 shows a diagrammatic representation of this situation which was considered by planners to be wasteful of land and untidy in appearance. Since 1945 efforts have been made to encourage a more compact form of urban growth. In addition, continued outward expansion has been limited by the introduction of measures to protect green space around cities. The latter involved the policy of creating Green Belts around major cities such as London, Birmingham, Leeds, Manchester and Newcastle. The Green Belt was designed to check the growth of cities thus preventing sprawl and also the encompassing of surrounding towns as the city grew. Further growth of conurbations would be stopped. A substantial rural zone was to be preserved around the cities, largely marking the urban limit at the end of the Second World War. Urban development in the form of 'infilling' and 'rounding off' could occur in towns or villages within the Green Belt but otherwise the land was meant to be used for agriculture and recreation and for a few special uses, e.g. cemeteries. Any breach of the Green Belt regulations, such as the building of housing, required the approval of the appropriate Secretary of State and this has proved to be a fairly rare occurrence. Apart from officially-designated Green Belts many urban planners have applied this thinking to other settlements even though a specific planned Green Belt has never been officially approved.

The policy has certainly affected the direction of urban growth since 1945. However, urban containment has proved to be a complex topic. Essential improvement to the quality of inner city areas inevitably caused pressure for urban growth because more than half of the population of redevelopment areas had to be rehoused elsewhere within the urban area. In addition, the trend towards suburban growth has continued. The

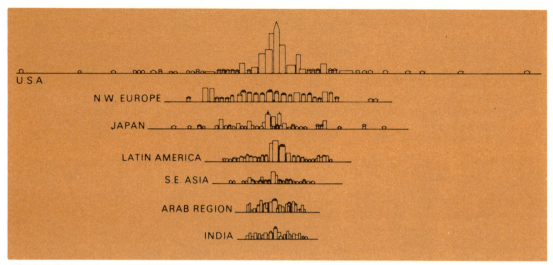

Fig. 5:6 *The form of cities in different parts of the world (MASAI). Compare the sprawling American city with the compact Indian city.*

combined effects of these processes was the invasion by urban growth of areas beyond the Green Belt in the shape of metropolitan villages, New Towns, expanded towns and other new or enlarged communities. Transport links had to be developed or improved between the major city and these settlements beyond the Green Belt. Such links inevitably had to cross the Green Belt, thereby introducing an urban-oriented land use and causing a change in the character of the rural zone. Another complication was the effect on the price of land within the urban area. Because the supply was now limited by the presence of a barrier, the Green Belt, it has been argued that this caused prices of available building land to escalate.

NEW TOWNS

In 1903 the Garden City Association started work on Letchworth. It was the first modern New Town in Britain in the sense that it was specifically planned to be a complete town. In 1920 a second example, Welwyn Garden City, was started. Most British New Towns date from the post-1946 period. In that year the New Towns Act became law and almost immediately several

New Towns were started. Fig. 5:7 lists the starting date and present population of the British New Towns.

New Towns and similar new planned settlements have been built in many countries. In some Scandinavian countries, they are suburbs rather than completely separate 'free-standing' towns. This is also true of most New Towns in America. Elsewhere the British type of New Town is more common. British New Towns occupy two sorts of situation, each of which has particular purposes.

Those near a major city are principally intended to aid the housing and environmental problems of the parent city. In order to achieve these aims, these New Towns, such as the ring around London, must provide an attractive living and working environment with a full range of types of employment, housing and services.

The second group of New Towns are intended to encourage economic development. They are often sited in regions suffering decline of traditional industries such as coal mining, e.g. Glenrothes, Peterlee, Washington. In both situations the objectives of creating a planned settlement include the organization of urban growth into

London Ring	Designated	Original Population	Population March 1980
Basildon	1949	25,000	98,000
Bracknell	1949	5,149	46,000
Crawley	1947	9,100	76,000
Harlow	1947	4,500	79,200
Hatfield	1948	8,500	26,000
Hemel Hempstead	1947	21,000	80,000
Stevenage	1946	6,700	73,500
Welwyn Garden City	1948	18,500	41,000
Milton Keynes	1967	40,000	90,000
Northampton	1968	133,000	156,000
Peterborough	1967	81,000	120,000
Others in England			
Aycliffe	1947	60	26,000
Central Lancashire (Preston-Chorley)	1970	234,500	253,500
Corby	1950	15,700	51,000
Peterlee	1948	200	25,500
Redditch	1964	32,000	61,800
Runcorn	1964	28,500	64,200
Skelmersdale	1961	10,000	39,300
Telford	1968	70,000	103,800
Warrington	1968	122,300	137,500
Washington	1964	20,000	53,230
Wales			
Cwmbran	1949	12,000	45,300
Newtown	1964	5,000	9,000
Scotland			
Cumbernauld	1955	3,000	50,443
East Kilbride	1947	2,400	75,800
Glenrothes	1948	1,100	37,000
Irvine	1966	34,600	59,070
Livingston	1962	2,100	37,060

Fig. 5:7 The population statistics of the British New Towns.

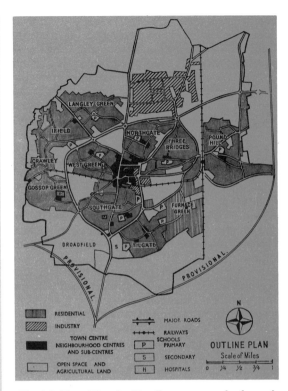

Fig. 5:8 Plan of Crawley New Town, an example of an early design for New Towns.

towns and the avoidance of sprawl. To avoid the process of 'creeping urbanization', in which towns, villages and agricultural land around major cities are swallowed up by unplanned growth, New Towns were intended to provide a focus for new growth. They were also planned to have a zone of peripheral green space to provide a barrier against encroachment by the expansion of adjoining communities.

Most British New Towns have been constructed on **green field sites**, that is in the country with perhaps a small existing village included within the site. As a result they have provided planners with an excellent opportunity to introduce new ideas about the design of towns and of particular parts of towns (housing areas, shopping centres, road systems, walkways, etc.). We have learned a great deal from this work and the lessons have

been applied in older settlements as well as in later New Towns.

Assignment
2   Compare, for example, the plan of an early New Town (Fig. 5:8) and a more recent New Town (Fig. 5:9). Make a list of the principal differences in design and appearance. Can you suggest reasons for the changes?

New Towns have not escaped criticism. Residents often complain that particular shops or other facilities are not present in the settlement. Ultimately, the explanation involves the question of threshold population. A major variety store may not consider that there are sufficient people in the town to ensure a viable threshold population for their store. Similarly, no one may be

Fig. 5:9 Plan of Livingston New Town, an example of a later design. Notice the change in design from winding streets to a grid or block pattern of major roads with separation of vehicles and pedestrians in the residential areas.

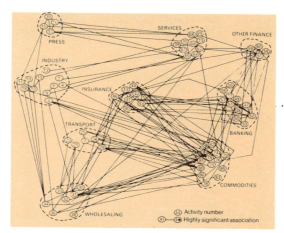

Fig. 5:10 Business connections, using taxi, different parts of the office districts of London (J. GODDARD).

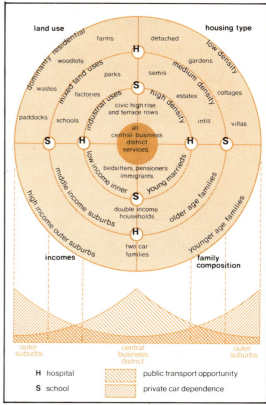

Fig. 5:11 Model of personal mobility in the city (M. HILLMAN and A. WHALLEY). The lower graph shows the relationship between car and public (bus/rail) transport.

willing to invest in a cinema or some other recreational facility because it is considered to be too risky. Part of the problem is that the New Town may not serve the size of hinterland which you might expect for a town of that size. In addition, people living in the New Town may travel to other centres, especially the nearest city, for shopping and the provision of services. Individual New Towns have also experienced problems at particular stages of development related to the level of transport provision and the distribution and adequacy of facilities such as shops or primary schools.

Some people would argue the New Towns merely organize urban growth and that they obviously do not prevent it. A considerable amount of urban growth was inevitable in Britain between 1945 and 1980 if improvements were to be made to housing and environmental conditions in the older districts of major cities. Perhaps a more realistic measure of the success of New Towns in the overall strategy of containing urban growth is to measure the degree of commuting to and from New Towns compared to internal movement within the New Town. This can be expressed as an **Index of Commuting**.

$$\text{Index} = \frac{\text{internal movement within New Town}}{\text{commuting to and commuting from New Town}}$$

A value above one would perhaps indicate success and a value of less than one would mean that commuting to and from the town was dominant. The original Garden City supporters would have expected very little commuting to and from New Towns. In reality, it is often quite substantial. But we must remember that considerable changes have occurred in transportation in the twentieth century, notably the widespread availability of the car for personal transport. In addition, there have been changes in the location of employment and of other facilities such as shops. As a result

modern patterns of movement are very complex (Fig. 5:10) and it is unreasonable to expect that an urban settlement of the size of a New Town could be completely self-contained.

Transport Issues

Apart from the movement of goods, most people need to travel on most days, either by walking, bus, bicycle, train or car. The distance involved in these journeys varies greatly from person to person.

Although suburbanization has occurred in the location of factories and offices, the city centre is still a major location of employment in Britain

87

and, indeed, in many other countries. The dispersal of population to peripheral estates and to dormitory settlements has raised a number of issues about the provision of transport and transport facilities in cities. Fig. 5:11 is a model by Hillman and Whalley of personal mobility in the city which relates land use zones, personal mobility, family income and composition and public and private transport. Figs. 5:12a, 5:12b, and 5:12c show the levels of car ownership in 1971 in Liverpool, Birmingham and London. Notice that the pattern in London resembles the private car dependence graph in the model (Fig. 5:11). Thus in London the level of car ownership increases with distance from the city centre. In the other two cities, car ownership is quite high in most suburban wards but the pattern is more complex than that for London. Car ownership is partly related to income, so ownership levels are normally lower in areas of below average income. Such areas often include some peripheral local authority housing estates. Another complicating factor is the exact relationship between the distribution of housing and places of employment.

In some cities, new peripheral industrial estates are close to large local authority housing areas. Workers may be able to walk or cycle to work. Two further possibilities are (1) car-sharing, that is three or four people travel to work in one car, (2) the use of public transport. Clearly, with many parts of major cities recording low levels of car ownership, public transport is an essential source of movement for many people.

One issue is that as people switch to private transport the viability of public transport is endangered. A cycle starts of rising fares and reduced services which in turn causes more people to seek alternative transport leading to further fare increases and service cuts and so on. However, in many developed countries there has been a reaction to this situation in recent years. In part it stems from an appreciation that some people are dependent upon public transport and that their personal mobility could become seriously curtailed (unable to travel to work) if the process went unchecked. There are many aspects of the problem. For example, fares tend to increase with

distance travelled in a series of steps or stages. This may discourage people living near the city centre from seeking employment in new peripheral industrial estates or office complexes. Some cities operate a fixed fare regardless of distance.

A second reason for increased concern about public transport relates to the impact of commuting, particularly by car, upon cities. This involves pollution from car exhausts and problems of congestion and parking and the costly provision of remedies in the form of ring roads, freeways, traffic-management systems and parking facilities. Apart from the building cost, many of these remedies have additional social costs and disruption costs. Houses or other buildings may have to be cleared to provide a path for an urban motorway. A further corridor of properties now suffers from the noise and pollution of a busy road. Residents and conservationists have reacted to the environmental impact of these roads.

Many plans for elaborate systems of urban motorways, such as the proposals for 'box' pat-

Fig. 5:12a Car ownership, Liverpool 1971.

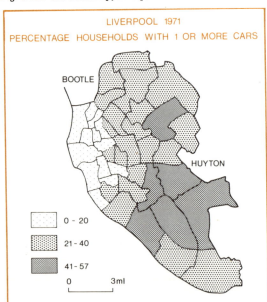

Fig. 5:12b Car ownership, Birmingham 1971.

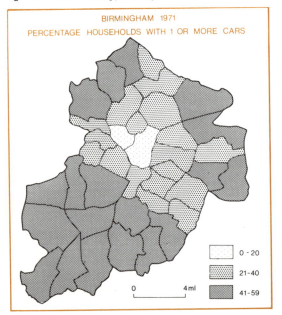

Fig. 5:12c Car ownership, London 1971.

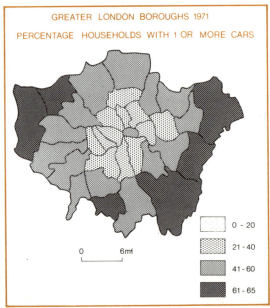

terns in London (Fig. 5:13) have been shelved or abandoned. In part this is a recognition of opposition to these schemes. It also indicates a reassessment of probable levels of car ownership and of commuting by private transport. Planners are also trying to redirect more commuting to public transport.

Nonetheless congestion does occur in cities and planners must deal with problems of movement and congestion at destinations or on the routes of journeys. Parking problems have led to a variety of schemes. Within the central area parking is controlled by charging for space and limiting the availability of space. Parking meters and car parks are commonplace as are the wardens who ensure that the rules are obeyed. When residential areas are located near the city centre space may have to be allocated for parking only by residents. Elsewhere within the city centre parking can be prevented by restrictions such as yellow-lines.

A section of ring road may aid the overall transport strategy by easing congestion at bottleneck junctions and diverting through traffic from the city centre.

A further major part of the overall transport policy is the improvement of public transport. London has an extensive underground system (Fig. 5:14). Much of the system was built early in the present century but recently new lines have been opened, e.g. the Victoria and Jubilee lines and the extension to Heathrow Airport. The substantial investment in these ventures illustrates the continued importance of mass transport systems of this kind. Indeed, many major cities have recently invested in subway systems. In addition several cities, e.g. Paris and Moscow, have had networks for many years. Other cities, such as Glasgow, have refurbished existing network and linked the system into a broader and more comprehensive transport network (Figs. 5:15 and 5:16).

The densely populated state of Hong Kong provides an excellent example of the varied methods which have been used to provide mass transport ranging from the mass transit railway with its sixteen stations to trams and ferries (Fig. 5:17).

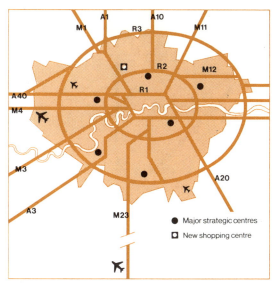

Fig. 5:13 Urban motorway proposals, London 1971.

- ● Major strategic centres
- □ New shopping centre

Trams were once a common feature of public transport in British cities. They were abandoned some twenty years ago in favour of buses although tram enthusiasts continue to urge their re-introduction. The cost of relaying track makes this unlikely. They do continue to operate in Hong Kong and some European cities, like Vienna, but the presence of tram-cars in the middle of city streets does cause problems for motor transport. The trams are driven by electricity so they do not cause pollution. They are also more suited to the constant stopping to uplift and set down passengers (which increases fuel consumption of buses). Frequent stops are an essential feature of urban transport.

Other transport policies include: (1) bus-lanes which give exclusive use of a lane to buses at peak periods; (2) park and ride schemes, where free parking is offered to entice commuters to park at the edge of the city centre and travel by bus or train; (3) tidal flow schemes where instead of having a four-lane road always divided into two equal flows (two towards the centre and two in the opposite direction), the direction of traffic in

lanes is adjusted at particular times of the day. For example, all lanes may be for city-bound traffic in the morning rush-hour and for traffic leaving the city in the evening rush-hour. These measures greatly increase the rate of movement although they can sometimes merely move the bottleneck outwards by a few kilometres unless other roads can cope with the faster flow or the traffic begins to disperse into smaller flows to particular destinations.

In an attempt to avoid congestion spots many motorists take alternative minor roads which often pass through residential areas. In order to protect these areas transport planners have sealed off entry to many minor roads (Fig. 5:18). One consequence is that the major roads must bear the full strain of peak traffic flows without undue congestion and confusion. Schemes to assist the free movement of such roads include a complete ban on street parking at peak hours, computer operated traffic lights and restrictions on traffic crossing the main directions of movement, e.g. turning right in Britain or left in France or Italy.

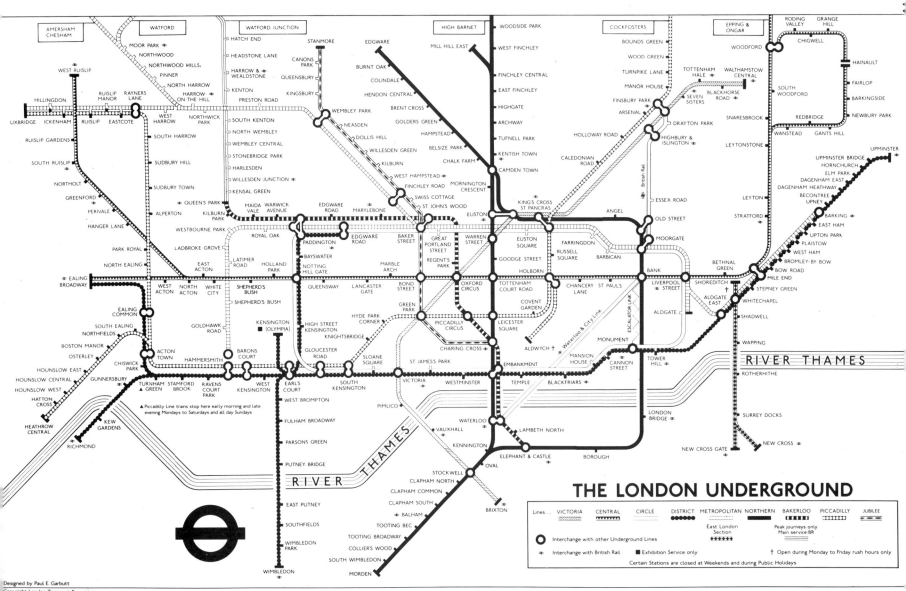

Fig. 5:14 *Topological map: the London Underground network.*

Fig. 5:15 *The refurbished electric underground system, Glasgow.*

Assignment

5 Local authorities announce their budgets in February or March. Examine the proposals for your local authority. Can you suggest any possible geographical effects which may result from the proposals? (e.g. school closures and effect on the catchment areas for schools).

With the present high levels of unemployment in Britain and most developed countries, the topic of employment is certainly an issue in society. To the extent that Britain is an urban society, the issue is therefore related to urban settlements, although urban settlements do not cause unemployment. The general level of unemployment in a country is a reflection of the rate of economic activity. That, in turn, depends upon the demand for goods and services within a country and in foreign markets. Apart from political and moral questions about the need to provide employment for people, there are also issues related to the uneven distribution of unemployment in the short- and long-term. Some parts of Britain and some districts of cities have had high levels of unemployment for many years. This can seriously affect the economic and social life of such areas and it seems to result in further social and environmental problems (vandalism, health problems, untidy built environment, etc.). We will return to these topics later.

In many developing countries, there seems to be a paradox in the substantial rural-urban migration, in the sense that many migrants cannot be certain of securing a job in the city. Employment opportunities take many forms, of which a thirty-five-hour, five-days-a-week job in a factory, office or shop is only one version. Part-time, or seasonal employment can be important in many cities in Third World countries. Of even greater importance is the rôle of traditional industries, or what is called the informal sector. This includes workshop and handicraft industries. A recent study of Abidjan in Ivory Coast concluded that 31 per cent of employment in 1970 was in the informal sector. Small firms continue to be very important sources of urban employment in many Third World Countries.

Economic Issues

These problems can be grouped into two categories, finance and employment.

Local authorities need income to pay for the various services which they provide. In Britain there are two main sources of this income, local rates and support from national government. You might imagine from controversy about the level of rates that it was the major source. In fact, it provides about one-third of the money with the remainder coming from government funds. Escalating rates may cause hardship and lead to the closure of some firms. Differences in rates can encourage location in a comparatively low rate area as opposed to a high rate area. In general, the impact of both trends is limited in Britain because most of the money comes from national funds. In some countries, such as the United States, the main source of money for local authorities is through local taxes. Major cities with expensive services can have problems raising sufficient money because the more affluent suburbs are located in the tax hinterland of a different authority. When the major city becomes unbalanced in terms of the social and economic characteristics of the population, so that it has a very large percentage of low income residents and of people needing specialized services, then there is a serious problem of financing. On these occasions state and federal aid must be made available to help balance the accounts of the city.

Another aspect of finance is the selection of the level of spending for each service or item in the budget. Cities have a particular amount of money available to pay for all services in that year and decisions must then be made about the amount spent on each activity. To some extent these decisions are shaped by legislation such as that relating to the provision of education in Britain to everyone between the ages of five and sixteen. But others, such as size of classes, range of subjects, quality of materials, provision of meals or location of schools, are all subject to possible discussion and adjustment in terms of funding. The same comments apply to all aspects of the budget. In reaching a decision about a new project councils will consider questions relating to the cost and to the neeed for that development.

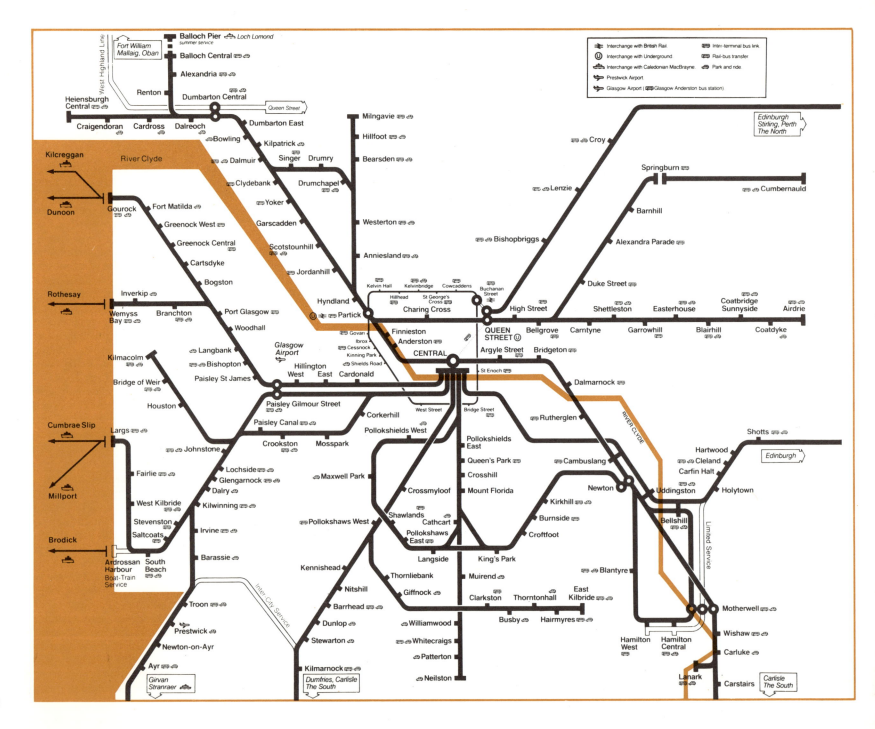

Balloch Pier — *Loch Lomond summer service*
Balloch Central
Alexandria

Fort William Mallaig, Oban

West Highland Line

Renton
Dumbarton Central
Queen Street

Heiensburgh Central

Craigendoran   Cardross   Dalreoch
Dumbarton East
Bowling   Kilpatrick
Milngavie
Croy
Edinburgh Stirling, Perth The North

Kilcreggan
Dunoon
River Clyde
Dalmuir   Singer   Drumry
Clydebank
Yoker
Drumchapel
Hillfoot
Bearsden
Springburn
Cumbernauld
Lenzie
Barnhill

Gourock   Fort Matilda
Greenock West
Greenock Central
Cartsdyke
Bogston
Garscadden
Scotstounhill
Westerton
Bishopbriggs
Alexandra Parade
Duke Street
Jordanhill
Anniesland

Rothesay
Inverkip
Wemyss Bay   Branchton
Port Glasgow
Woodhall
Hyndland
Kelvin Hall   Kelvinbridge   Cowcaddens
Hillhead   St George's Cross   Buchanan Street
Partick
Charing Cross
High Street
Shettleston   Easterhouse
Coatbridge Sunnyside
Airdrie

Kilmacolm
Langbank
Bishopton
Glasgow Airport
Govan
Ibrox
Cessnock
Kinning Park
Shields Road
Finnieston
Anderston
QUEEN STREET
Bellgrove   Carntyne   Garrowhill   Blairhill   Coatdyke
Bridge of Weir
Hillington West   East   Cardonald
CENTRAL
Argyle Street
Bridgeton
Houston
Paisley St James
Paisley Gilmour Street
West Street   Bridge Street
St Enoch
Dalmarnock
RIVER CLYDE

Cumbrae Slip
Largs
Paisley Canal
Corkerhill
Pollokshields West
Rutherglen
Shotts
Johnstone
Crookston   Mosspark
Pollokshields East
Queen's Park
Cambuslang
Hartwood
Cleland
Carfin Halt
Edinburgh

Fairlie
Lochside
Glengarnock
Dalry
Maxwell Park
Crosshill
Mount Florida
Newton
Uddingston
Holytown
Limited Service

Millport
West Kilbride
Kilwinning
Crossmyloof
Kirkhill
Burnside
Croftfoot
Bellshill

Brodick
Stevenston
Saltcoats
Pollokshaws West
Shawlands   Cathcart
Pollokshaws East
Langside   King's Park
Blantyre

Ardrossan Harbour
Boat-Train Service
South Beach
Barassie
Kennishead
Thornliebank
Muirend
Hamilton West
Hamilton Central
Motherwell

Inter City Service
Nitshill
Giffnock
Clarkston   Thorntonhall
East Kilbride
Wishaw

Troon
Barrhead
Williamwood
Busby   Hairmyres
Carluke

Prestwick
Dunlop
Whitecraigs
Newton-on-Ayr
Stewarton
Patterton
Lanark
Carstairs

Ayr
Kilmarnock
Neilston

Girvan Stranraer
Dumfries, Carlisle The South
Carlisle The South

Legend:
Interchange with British Rail.
Interchange with Underground.
Interchange with Caledonian MacBrayne.
Prestwick Airport.
Glasgow Airport
Inter-terminal bus link.
Rail-bus transfer.
Park and ride.
Glasgow Anderston bus station).

92

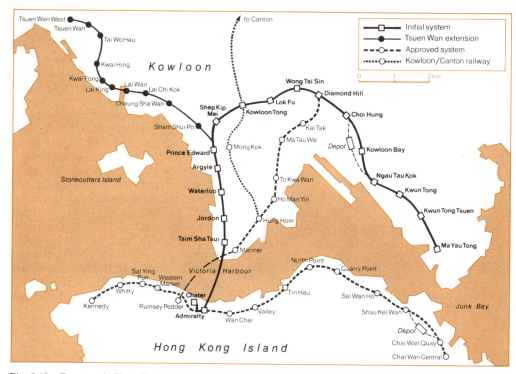

to Canton

	Initial system
	Tsuen Wan extension
	Approved system
	Kowloon/Canton railway

0 1 2 km

Kowloon

Tsuen Wan West
Tsuen Wan
Tai Wo Hau
Kwai Hing
Kwai Fong
Lai Wan
Lai King
Lai Chi Kok
Cheung Sha Wan
Sham Shui Po
Shep Kip Mei
Kowloon Tong
Lok Fu
Wong Tai Sin
Diamond Hill
Choi Hung
Kai Tak
Ma Tau Wai
Depot
Kowloon Bay
Ngau Tau Kok
Kwun Tong
Kwun Tong Tsuen
Ma Yau Tong
Mong Kok
Prince Edward
Argyle
Waterloo
To Kwa Wan
Ho Man Yin
Hung Hom
Jordon
Tsim Sha Tsui
Mariner

Stonecutters Island

North Point
Quarry Point
Sai Ying Pun
Western Market
Whitty
Rumsey Pedder
Chater
Kennedy
Admiralty
Wan Chai
Valley
Tin Hau
Sai Wan Ho
Shau Kei Wan
Depot
Chai Wan Quay
Chai Wan Central

Junk Bay

Victoria Harbour

Hong Kong Island

Fig. 5:17a Transport in Hong Kong: The new mass transit railway network.

Fig. 5:17b Trams in central Hong Kong.

*Fig. 5:17c
The Hong Kong mass transit railway
near Kowloon Bay Station.*

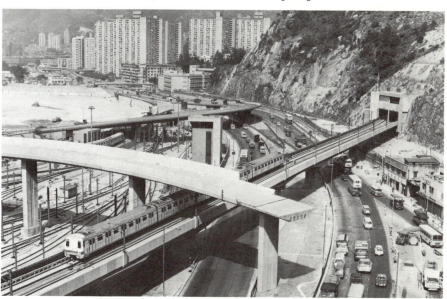

*Opposite – Fig. 5:16
The Trans-Clyde integrated transport system. Note the connection
points between different forms of transport.*

Fig. 5:18 Street closure to prevent residential areas becoming major traffic routes.

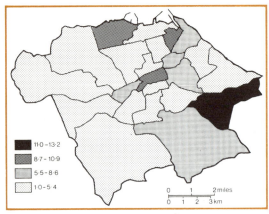

11·0 – 13·2
8·7 – 10·9
5·5 – 8·6
1·0 – 5·4

0   1   2 miles
0   1   2   3 km

Fig. 5:19 Overcrowding (more than 1.5 persons per room), Edinburgh 1971.

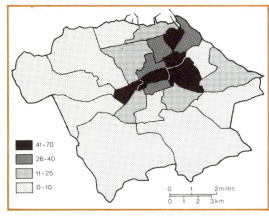

41 – 70
26 – 40
11 – 25
0 – 10

0   1   2 miles
0   1   2   3 km

Fig. 5:20 Households which share or lack a bath, Edinburgh 1971.

Another aspect of urban employment in the Third World is the temporary migration of males for part of a year or for several years, while the rest of the family remains in the traditional rural village. For example this type of migration has become associated with mining in various parts of Africa. There are issues related to the disruption of family life and the living conditons in the mining camps. An example in developed countries would be workers at remote building sites or on offshore oil production platforms.

Housing Issues

In Chapter 4 the principal sources of housing in Britain were described. At the start of the twentieth century there was a problem of supply in the sense that there were not enough houses for every family to have a house. Although many houses were built after 1919 the population of Britain also grew. In addition, there were periods when building virtually stopped, e.g. during the Second World War. In some settlements many houses were damaged or destroyed during that War, e.g. London, Coventry and Clydebank. Age also took a toll and many nineteenth-century properties became decayed and very inadequate in terms of amenities and standards. Two aspects

of inadequate housing are overcrowding (Fig. 5:19) and the absence of facilities such as toilets or baths (Fig. 5:20). The latter mainly occurs in areas of older housing near the centre of cities but overcrowding is found in both central and certain more peripheral locations. In Britain we define overcrowding as more than 1.5 persons per room. Thus, a concentration of large families in relatively standard size local authority houses can produce an area of overcrowding on our maps. Equally, overcrowding can result from insufficient housing, in total or at a particular rent,

leading people to share with relatives. A further reason for overcrowding is based upon economic factors. Several students, for example, may share a flat. This helps to reduce the cost of the rent for each individual. Similarly, people may have lodgers to help supplement the cost of housing or assist the family income. You can appreciate, therefore, that overcrowding is not always an easy problem to resolve. Certainly it is much more complex than the problem of bad quality housing. The solution to bad housing is either demolition (**redevelopment**) or improvement (**rehabilitation**). Substantial portions of the inner city areas in most British cities have been cleared at some point during the past two decades in the pursuit of redevelopment. After a temporary phase of dereliction with large vacant areas, new housing is constructed at a lower density and to a higher level of amenity than the housing which previously occupied the site. Many schemes in the 1960s and 1970s included several multi-storey developments.

Redevelopment is both costly and disruptive of existing communities. An alternative strategy when buildings are fairly sound is the process of rehabilitation (Figs. 5:21a and 5:21b). The external appearance is improved by cleaning, sandblasting and plasterwork and new windows and doors are fitted. Inside the buildings new fittings are installed and a small number of larger flats result from the rehabilitation process. Untidy and unsightly gardens are landscaped and redesigned to give play areas, drying space for clothes and screened areas for the storage of rubbish bins.

In the post-1945 period the housing problems in the inner areas of major cities such as Birmingham, Liverpool, Manchester and Glasgow had become so acute that vigorous action was required. In every case many districts were demolished and the residents were moved to peripheral estates, New Towns or to other urban settlements through overspill agreements. These agreements were drawn up between the parent city and the foster settlements and involved anything from a few dozen to several thousand families being rehoused in the foster settlement. Normally the settlements accepting large numbers of overspill families had a demand for

Fig. 5:21a Rehabilitation of tenements.

*Fig. 5:21b
Rehabilitation of the back courts of tenements.*

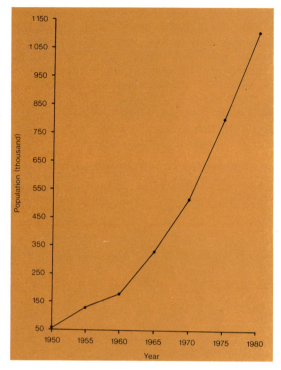

Fig. 5:22 Population growth, Abidjan, Ivory Coast.

workers because a new large factory had opened, e.g. a car factory in the 1960s such as the one which recently closed at Linwood to the west of Paisley.

HOUSING IN DEVELOPING COUNTRIES

Massive migration of people from rural to urban areas places great strains upon the ability of the urban settlements to house the new residents. Britain experienced these probelms in the nineteenth century but many developing countries have only recently been faced with this dilemma.

Abidjan, Ivory Coast, illustrates this situation. Rapid population increase (Fig. 5:22) has affected the structure of residential areas in the city (Fig. 5:23). A recent International Labour Office study (1976) said: 'From the point of view of the physical environment, Abidjan's growth has been closely supervised and presents few symptoms of strained capacity affecting the population as a whole, except with regard to sewage disposal. Abidjan prides itself on being an exceptionally well designed city; however, while it provides an extremely congenial habitat for the car-owning classes, this high standard has to a certain extent been achieved at the expense of poorer inhabitants.'

The report notes that the provision of low rent housing has not kept pace with population growth and, as a result, recent migrants have erected huts in shanty towns or squatter developments. Indeed by 1970 about one quarter of the city's population lived in shanty towns. These squatter areas are unsanitary, overcrowded and lack proper facilities such as reliable water supplies, sewage disposal, lighting and proper streets and paths.

The proportion of the population living in shanty towns varies from one developing country to another. Whilst it is generally substantial it is not total. In other words there are areas of better housing in all Third World cities. Equally, in some countries such as India, shanty towns or squatter areas do not represent the worst housing conditions. In these cases the residents of squatter settlements are often more established urban migrants who have managed to climb at least one rung up the housing ladder in the city.

In 1971 it was estimated by the United Nations that one thousand million people were living in substandard housing. The highest percentages of people living in slums or uncontrolled settlements (shanty towns) was 80 per cent in Buenaventura in Colombia. Many Third World cities had at least 25 per cent of their inhabitants living in this type of housing area. Figs. 5:24a-c illustrate the conditions in these areas.

Shanty towns are known by various names depending upon the country, e.g. barrio (Colombia), barriodas (Peru), ranchos (Venezuela), favelas (Brazil), bustees (India), sarifas (Iraq) and bidonvilles (housing North Africans on the edge of major French cities such as Paris and Marseilles). Although the problem of standards and environmental quality are almost overwhelming in these areas, perhaps the most serious issue is the fact that the inhabitants of squatter settlements have no legal right to their shack or the land on which it stands.

Self-help is one path to improvement. Bryan Roberts in 1978 wrote that in parts of Rio de Janeiro, 'the process of housing improvement has reached a point where the settlements are hardly distinguishable from legal housing areas with a reasonably good standard of housing'. Groups of neighbours or individual families improve the houses and instal water supplies and drains for sewage.

Hong Kong is an excellent example of a country which has taken extensive measures to cope with the problem of squatter areas. Massive resettlement estates, some accommodating more than 100 000 people, have been the main source of new housing. Much of the housing is in multi-storey blocks because of the pressures on space in Hong Kong. The authorities have also introduced strict regulations in order to restrict new squatting. Even in Hong Kong the success of the actions is threatened by the scale of migration. Yet Hong Kong has many advantages when compared to most Third World cities. The most important advantage is the economic growth which the country is enjoying. This provides money to invest in resettlement schemes and slum clearance projects. Elsewhere, projects are often on a more modest scale as Fig. 5:25 illustrates with reference to 'mini-houses' in Colombia.

Fig. 5:23 Plan of Abidjan.

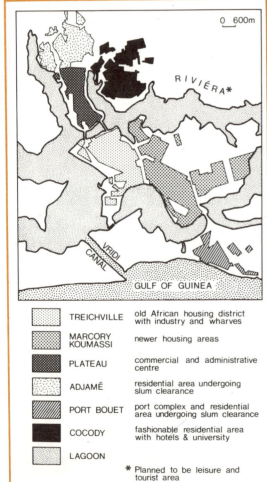

	TREICHVILLE	old African housing district with industry and wharves
	MARCORY KOUMASSI	newer housing areas
	PLATEAU	commercial and administrative centre
	ADJAMÉ	residential area undergoing slum clearance
	PORT BOUET	port complex and residential area undergoing slum clearance
	COCODY	fashionable residential area with hotels & university
	LAGOON	

* Planned to be leisure and tourist area

Fig. 5:24a Shanty housing, the swamp area, Rio de Janeiro.

Fig. 5:24b Shanty housing, Lusaka, Zambia.

Fig. 5:24c Pavement dwellers, Calcutta.

Fig. 5:25 Planned provision of cheap mini-houses, Medellin, Colombia.

In many Third World cities there are two basic locations of squatter settlements. First, on the periphery where land is most readily available. This is especially true where the land is not used because it is too steep or marshy or unsuited in other ways to agriculture or commercial land use. Second, more central locations. Clearly there are problems in obtaining sites but where they are available the situation is almost ideal because it is near the main places of employment. These centrally located shanty areas mean a saving in transport costs and a better chance of getting and keeping a job because travel-to-work is simpler.

What does the future hold for squatter settlements? If rates of population increase or urban migration remains high the prospects of rapid improvements in conditions and facilities are probably bleak. A study of the attitudes of squatters in Lima in 1970 to the levels of provision of services found that the greatest dissatisfactions were: (a) the insecurity of property titles (ownership of house and land), (b) the provision of medical services and amenities such as street paving or services such as policing. People sought a sense of security and improvements in their environment.

A practical course of action by many governments would be the provision of essential facilities such as water and sewage disposal and the creation of a framework of house plots. If cheap building materials were then made available, a semi-controlled low rent housing section would develop spontaneously (in the same way that squatter settlements do at present). The advantages would be the provision, from the outset, of basic facilities and the introduction of a relatively inexpensive form of town planning without causing problems of the schemes costing too much money.

Environmental and Social Issues

Air and water pollution both detract from the quality of the environment. In Britain legislation exists which controls the permitted level of pollution by man of rivers and of the atmosphere. The dangers of deaths from 'smogs' led to the introduction of smokeless zones in urban areas in Britain. Smoke, soot and dust particles tended to increase the duration and frequency of fogs in winter in major British cities (e.g. London and Glasgow). Recently there has been a marked decrease in the number of days of fog in these cities because of the restrictions on the emission of smoke. However, pollution still occurs. Indeed, with the use of new chemicals and industrial materials we must always remain alert to the dangers of atmospheric and water pollution. At present, the main focus of attention in developed countries has turned to the question of the pollution of rivers, lakes, seas and oceans. In addition to the dangers to fresh water supplies and health risks to people living near polluted waterways, there is also a major threat to marine and river life (plants, fish, insects and animals).

Further environmental hazards include the possibility of flooding and abnormal noise levels such as those experienced by people living near motorways or under the flight path of major airports. Special protective measures may be required. For example, houses close to airports and in direct line of the flight path need additional soundproofing to make the noise level tolerable.

Marked differences occur in the geography of diseases. Some parts of cities have high levels of occurrence whereas other areas have comparatively low levels (Fig. 5:26). The degree of high risk varies according to the characteristics of the urban environment. This may depend upon physical factors such as water quality or human features such as life style. Other risks also vary from one part of the city to another, e.g. the frequency of house fires.

Apart from housing and employment, the principal social issues can be grouped into two types: (1) problems of access, (2) problems of conflict or tension. Issues about access involve the spatial distribution of facilities, e.g. shops, community centres, sports centres, play areas, nursery schools, etc. These facilities are often unevenly distributed in cities. For example, in many British cities the emphasis in the 1950s and 1960s was on building houses and other facilities had a low priority. The level of provision was very limited with a lack of variety of shops. The concentration of these facilities at a small number of locations meant that people in certain parts of housing estates were very remote from the facilities.

Increasingly it is appreciated that problems of access vary from person to person. Disabled people, for example, have particular problems unless special provision is made for them in the design of facilities. There may be very little additional cost if the question of access for disabled people is part of the initial planning of shopping centres or

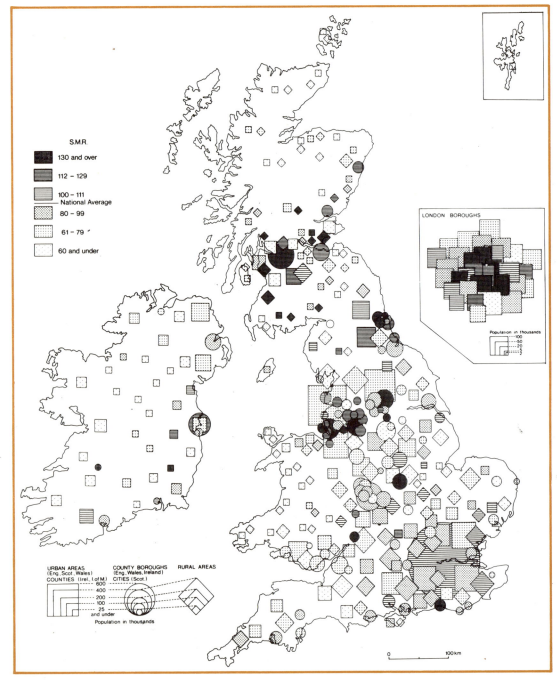

S.M.R.

- ■ 130 and over
- ▦ 112 – 129
- ▤ 100 – 111
  National Average
- ▦ 80 – 99
- ▫ 61 – 79
- □ 60 and under

LONDON BOROUGHS

Population in thousands
100
50
20

URBAN AREAS
(Eng.,Scot.,Wales)
COUNTIES (Irel., I.of M.)
600
400
200
100
25
and under
Population in thousands

COUNTY BOROUGHS
(Eng.,Wales,Ireland)
CITIES (Scot.)

RURAL AREAS

0   100 km

other facilities but subsequent conversion can be quite expensive. Similarly, other groups of people may be limited in terms of personal mobility, e.g. the elderly or those with no private transport or limited incomes. The latter, for example, affects the amount of money which can be spent on transport and this, in turn, may affect the ability of the person to visit a sports centre or some other facility.

Crimes against persons or property are examples of social conflict in which the criminals break the rules of society. Where the risk of assault, vandalism or theft becomes unacceptably high, a form of environmental pollution occurs. Visible aspects are walls covered in graffiti, broken windows and vandalized abandoned cars. Fear of attack or burglary are further aspects of this environmental problem. People may press for additional policing or more rigorous action against offenders. They may also take precautions such as installing burglar alarms or car alarms. Particular groups can be especially at risk, e.g. the elderly.

Tensions can develop between neighbours or between different groups in urban communities. Disputes between neighbours are often short-lived but when they persist one party may ultimately decide to move to another area. Their ability to do this can be restricted by cost or by the availability of another house. Local authority tenants must seek a transfer and they may have to wait for a long time before their request can be granted. A long wait is particularly common when there is a large number of people waiting to be allocated a local authority house for the first time.

Conflicts or tensions between groups in a community mostly involve differences in religion or in ethnic characteristics. The latter are frequently referred to by the term **racial conflict**. Northern Ireland provides an example of conflict which is linked to religious differences. Racial conflicts

Fig. 5:26 Female deaths from Cancer of the Lung or Bronchus (G. M. HOWE).

include the segregation of white and black townships in South Africa. The recent riots in the large black township of Soweto illustrate racial tensions which primarily result from many of the black residents feeling that they are underprivileged members of society.

In Britain, there are distinctive ethnic communities in several cities, e.g. inner London, Bradford, Bristol and Birmingham. The presence of people of a different colour, religion or ethnic background need not, and does not, inevitably lead to conflict. When the group suffers discrimination then resentment and frustration can create tension and produce the potential flashpoint for conflict. Equally when the majority group in the original population feels their jobs or housing standards threatened, they may discriminate against the newcomers, and the seeds of conflict are sown. In these situations racial conflict overlaps with issues about access; access to jobs or houses which are in demand and in short supply.

In 1977 there were about 1.77 million coloured people in Britain of Commonwealth origin. Most migrants had come from the West Indies, India and Pakistan. The majority of these migrants lived in London and the West Midlands. In the United States residential areas tend to be segregated on the basis of ethnic origin (white suburbs, black inner city areas). In Britain, this type of spatial segregation is less clearly defined. This may be a consequence of the difference in size of the coloured population in American and British cities. In some American cities more than half of the population is coloured, e.g. Washington DC, whereas in Britain this level of segregation only occurs in quite small portions of the city. P. N. Jones in a study of ethnic areas in Birmingham found that in 1971 the coloured population was associated with a zone of by-law housing which had become unattractive to established local residents. Similarly, the Pakistani community in Glasgow is principally associated with certain tenement districts. Thus these ethnic areas tend to be located in the inner city, a zone with generally poor housing conditions and an unattractive environment, characterized by decayed buildings and large areas of derelict land.

These features can reinforce the feelings of younger members that the group is underprivileged and disadvantaged. Yet one possible solution, rehousing in peripheral local authority estates, may be opposed because of fears of isolation and the desire to maintain contact with others who share their culture and beliefs. Understanding and mutual respect provide the basis of long-term harmony but this takes time and requires a willingness to seek that end. The situation is further complicated by the fact that inevitable tensions between people readily acquire an extra dimension if religious or ethnic differences are involved.

Assignment

6 The issues discussed in this chapter often appear in local and national newspapers. Make a file of newspaper cuttings for a month which refers to the issues discussed in the chapter. Which issues were of (a) local (b) national importance? If the answer to (a) was different from that for (b), how would you explain the difference?

Revision Questions

1 Give examples of the types of problems common to urban areas under the following headings:
 (a) Physical
 (b) Economic
 (c) Environmental
 (d) Social
2 What factors affect the level of demand for housing in city areas?
3 Communication within cities can create several difficulties for its inhabitants. Discuss the main difficulties and the efforts made to overcome them.
4 How does the time element affect major issues in cities? e.g. planning measures or communication networks.

5 Why is urban growth or sprawl a cause of concern to city planners and local authorities?
6 How is urban sprawl curtailed?
7 List the main differences between New Towns and other urban areas in Britain. Explain why such towns are necessary.
8 Why should the level of car ownership increase as you move away from the city centre? What other factors affect the number of people in cities who own cars?
9 How do city authorities resolve the problems created by:
 (a) Movement of persons from home to work.
 (b) Pollution due to industrial and traffic fumes.
 (c) Fast movement of traffic through cities.
10 What are the following? Describe their effect on city traffic problems:
 (a) Ring roads
 (b) Bus lanes
 (c) Restricted access
 (d) Pedestrian zones
 (e) Park and ride schemes
 (f) Tidal flow schemes.
11 List the main services provided by local authorities. How are these services paid for?
12 Why are people attracted to urban areas from rural areas in developing countries? Why are these migrants so often disappointed when they reach the cities?
13 What kinds of problems do these migrants create for cities in developing countries?
14 What are shanty towns? Where and why do they exist?

15 How have governments (local and national) tackled the problems of overcrowding and sub-standard housing in British cities?
16 Describe the chief cause of the following environmental issues:
 (a) Atmospheric pollution
 (b) Noise pollution
 (c) Health risks from poor sanitation
 (d) Access to services.
17 What kind of problems arise from racial and religious conflicts in cities? Illustrate your answer by referring to any known examples.

CHAPTER SIX
RURAL SETTLEMENT

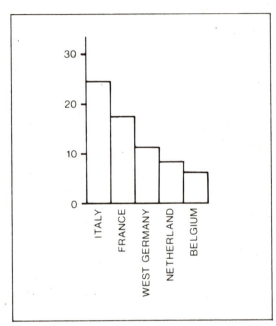

Fig. 6:1 *Percentage employed in agriculture in five E.E.C. countries.*

If the study of **Urban settlement** is accepted as the study of towns and cities it may seem rather obvious to say that the study of **Rural settlement** is the study of smaller settlement units, viz. farm-steads, hamlets and villages. However, it is not quite as simple as that. Many towns and cities are surrounded by an area which is still partly rural but although many of the residents live in the country, they are not socially and economically part *of* it. In effect, many countryside settlements are gradually being urbanized and it is becoming increasingly difficult to differentiate between urban and rural in such areas. The characteristics of villages are changing in many ways. New residential estates house people who commute daily from rural to city areas for employment. These people have moved out from urban areas into the rural districts and colonized settlements, changing their character from agricultural villages to dormitory suburbs and commuter villages. The rural identity of these areas is therefore rapidly disappearing. We will return to the topic of these villages later in this chapter.

One reliable way of establishing the rural identity of a settlement is by referring to the employment structure. Settlements which have more than 50 per cent of the employed inhabitants engaged in agriculture in one form or another can claim with reasonable justification to be rural. As we have seen with the development of commuter settlements, fewer villages can make this claim in Britain. In European countries such as France, Spain and Denmark identifying rural settlement is perhaps easier since a greater part of the economies of these countries is based on agriculture. Fig. 6:1 shows the proportions of persons employed in agriculture for a group of selected

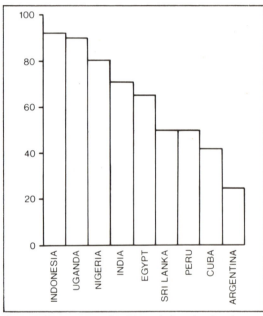

Fig. 6:2 *Percentage employed in agriculture in selected developing countries.*

countries in Western Europe. In Third World Countries most of the labour force is employed in farming (Fig. 6:2). The majority of the population of developing countries lives in rural settlements ranging from tiny hamlets widely dispersed throughout the countryside to larger market villages.

In most countries throughout the world, people are leaving rural areas for a variety of reasons.

Many are leaving farming occupations to seek new jobs in urban areas. The various reasons for this are examined in detail in a later section of this chapter.

Patterns of Rural Settlement

There are two basic patterns: nucleated and dispersed. Various factors favour the dominance of one pattern but the situation is often complex and contains elements of both types. Patterns can differ in similar physical environments because of historical factors such as landownership and levels of economic development. Dispersed farms are found in both fertile and hostile environments and in rich or poor areas.

The density of the pattern, measured by distance between farms or settlements, is partly due to fertility and partly to the type of farming and pressure of population.

NUCLEATION

Man tends to seek the company of others. He is gregarious. Clustering can mean that help is available in times of need. Services or equipment can be shared, e.g. expensive machinery.

In Chapter 4 seven shapes of villages were illustrated, each apparently influenced by transport routes. Thus accessibility may encourage nucleation. Farmers may seek other features in addition to access to surrounding fields and to markets. These include water, defendable sites or flood-free sites. A variety of factors, therefore, can produce nucleated villages. The factors can also reflect previous conditions as in the case of hilltop villages in Southern Italy. Originally sited for defence, the locations remain although that factor is no longer relevant.

The development of nucleated villages has been encouraged by the emergence or imposition of certain systems of landholding. In medieval Europe many farmers worked strips of land which were scattered over several fields. This favoured nucleation in villages where the centrality allowed the farmers to minimize the distance travelled to their strips.

Many Third World countries still show this type of situation. The sub-division of landholdings was furthered by inheritance whereby the land passed to a farmer's sons. Each son received part of the father's land. Many governments have sought a rationalization and reorganization of these divided fields in order to increase productivity. This alters the shapes of fields and strips and the pattern of landholding but nucleated villages normally remain as the characteristic settlements.

The Borde region of North-West Germany is a fine example of an area in which settlements are distributed in a nucleated (agglommerated) pattern. As Fig. 6:3 shows, the villages in this region are in fact nucleated both in terms of their physical structure and in terms of their spatial distribution. Indeed they are fairly regularly spaced in an approximately triangular pattern. Their form and distribution owe much to the physical environment which greatly influenced the pattern of agricultural development. The soils were fertile and this made the area highly attractive to early settlers. The farming system which was adopted involved the cultivation of strips which in turn encouraged nucleation of settlement. The centralized location of the farmer's house in the village had the advantage of minimizing the distances which the farmer had to travel daily to his strips which were scattered throughout the open fields. The village adopted the **Haufendorfer** form shown in Fig. 6:4a. It is interesting to note that there is a close similarity between the patterns of settlement evaluation in this region and

Fig. 6:3 The pattern of settlement in the Borde region, West Germany.

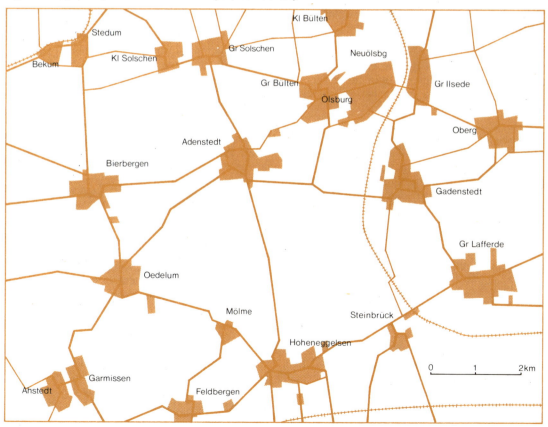

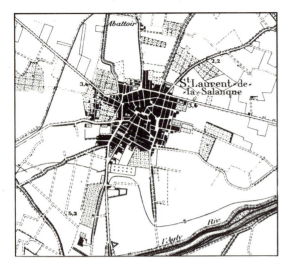

Fig. 6:4a *Haufendorf village in France, with a girdle of open fields and meadows beside the river.*

Fig. 6:4b *Planned farm settlement: Nord-Oost Polder, Holland.*

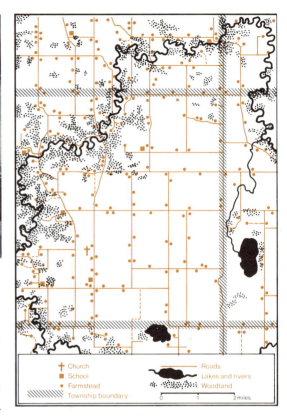

Church
School
Farmstead
Township boundary

Roads
Lakes and rivers
Woodland

0   1   2 miles

Fig. 6:5 *The pattern of settlement in rural Minnesota (after W. MEAD and E. BROWN).*

those found in East Anglia in England. This is probably because settlements in the latter area can trace their origins to the period of Anglo-Saxon colonization.

The location of nucleated settlements can be influenced by relief as, for example in the long, narrow valleys in South Wales. Local drainage characteristics may lead to linear arrangements, particularly at the junction of rocks of different permeability, e.g. chalk/clay or limestone/clay. Notable examples are found at the base of the scarp slopes of the Yorkshire Wolds, Lincoln Edge, Chilterns and Cotswolds. Artificial drainage in clay areas may also favour regular patterns of settlement, e.g. Fenlands, Polders.

DISPERSION

Man may prefer to live in communities but circumstances can favour a more dispersed pattern of settlement.

One set of conditions which produces dispersion relates to various environmental difficulties. Wherever the quality of land is poor (altitude, climate, soil), cultivation may be replaced by pastoral farming. This activity is generally associated with dispersed farms and often a relatively low population density. Pastoral farmers will seek particular sites with favourable qualities such as sheltered pastures, pockets of better land and accessibility to markets and to other areas.

Dispersed patterns also occur in areas of arable farming, e.g. the Wheatlands of Canada and the Great Plains of the U.S.A. Mechanization of farming activities there means that labour requirements are minimal. As a result these are sparsely populated areas with widely spaced large farms.

When land is reclaimed the new settlement can also produce a dispersed pattern, e.g. Holland's polderlands (Fig. 6:4b). Whether reclaimed from the sea or won from the forest or wilderness, a pioneer phase of settlement in colonizing these new agricultural areas may involve dispersed farms. Later the pattern may change and villages may develop.

COMPLEX PATTERNS

It is possible for elements of nucleation and dispersion to co-exist. In other words, there are a number of villages surrounded by a network of dispersed farms. This arrangement is common on lowland areas of Britain, e.g. Central and South-ern England or Central and Eastern Scotland or Northern Ireland.

On occasions change can occur from one system being dominant towards the other situation. With the enclosing of fields in the sixteenth, seventeenth and eighteenth centuries, nucleation was emphasized. Gradually the creation of tenant farmers in the nineteenth century led to a more dispersed pattern as farmers found it more convenient to be located on their farmland rather than travel daily from a village. In France, after the French Revolution, many large estates were divided into small plots and given to peasant farmers. This process encouraged the emergence of a dispersed pattern of rural settlements.

Fig. 6:6a The pattern of settlement in North Wales (based upon O.S. map of Snowdonia).

Fig. 6:6b The pattern of settlement in Cambridgeshire (based upon O.S. map of Cambridgeshire).

In the United States the Homestead Act (1860) created sections of farmland of approximately 65 hectares. A condition of the Act was that farmers had to work the land continuously in order to retain their homesteading. A dispersed pattern was an inevitable consequence of this system. Even buildings such as schools and churches were dispersed rather than grouped into a single settlement. As Fig. 6:5 shows the pattern still persists. There have been some changes. For example, many farmers have moved into small settlements. They have been attracted by the facilities available and are able to move because they are no longer compelled to live on their farm.

In some parts of the world, e.g. South-East Asia, Africa and South America, European colonization introduced a pattern of large estates and villages. With independence some countries have abolished these large estates and redistributed the land in smaller parcels to peasant farmers. This trend has favoured the introduction of dispersed settlement in particular regions although nucleated settlements also occur in developing countries, e.g. Bantu Kraals. This illustrates the dual influences of climate and level of economic development. From these examples we can see that widely varying social and economic conditions can create similar settlement patterns.

Assignment

1   Select a 1:50 000 O.S. sheet of a predominantly rural area. Take two different areas of the map each of 25 sq. km. (5 x 5). Cover each area in turn with tracing paper and plot all settlements (farms, houses, villages, etc.). Count the number of each type of settlement in each area. How would you describe the pattern of each area? How would you explain each pattern? (You should refer to factors such as relief, drainage, possible type of farming, accessibility, historical development.)

2   Study the distribution patterns shown in Figs. 6:6a (N. Wales) and 6:6b (Cambridgeshire). Which map is typical of (a) Nucleated (b) Dispersed distribution settlement pattern? Explain your choice. Suggest factors responsible for the particular pattern shown in each of the study areas.

Depopulation and Change

In many parts of the world a trend has been emerging for some time whereby rural areas are losing population in either relative or absolute

103

terms. Fig. 6:7 shows the trend in population growth in rural and urban areas in the United States from 1800 to 1970. The rates of growth are different with urban growth outpacing the increase in the population of rural areas. This trend is repeated in many countries although the rates vary in detail. Urban population growth is larger than rural growth in very different countries, e.g. Britain and India or Brazil. In addition, in some countries, e.g. Britain, France, U.S.A., the total number of people living in rural areas is declining.

Depopulation (the loss of population) can affect rural areas in a variety of ways. It can produce an imbalance in terms of population structure, e.g. many old people and few young people, more females than males. The loss of population can affect the quality of service provision and, indirectly, ultimately lead to the loss of some services. This section examines these trends and will also refer to other changes such as the impact of tourism on rural areas in some countries. This can produce a potential conflict of interests between the preservation of a landscape and way of life and the provision of leisure facilities and the invasion by the owners of second homes. These are owned by urban dwellers and used at week-ends or as holiday retreats and retirement residences.

RURAL DEPOPULATION

In the last two centuries many rural areas in Europe have suffered relative or absolute decline of population. Where numbers have increased the rate of growth has been less than that for urban areas, because of various historical, social and economic factors. The net result is that many rural areas are recognized as regions of **out-migration.** The principal examples of such regions in Europe are shown on Fig. 6:8.

In effect two forces acted simultaneously: rural push and urban attraction. Rural push resulted from unattractive features of the opportunities and facilities offered by rural areas. Progressively changes in farm technology and method have reduced the need for a large rural population. Many people became surplus to the requirements for rural labour. Sometimes the change was sud-

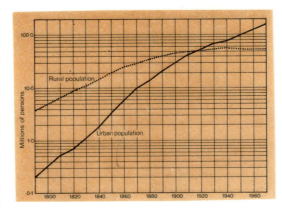

Fig. 6:7 *The proportions of urban and rural residents in the U.S.A. 1790-1970.*

den, dramatic and painful as in the Highland Clearances with thousands of Highland Scots being displaced when sheep farming was introduced in place of more traditional agriculture and cattle rearing.

Natural catastrophe can also create dramatic and comparatively sudden intense pressure in the form of rural push. Crop failures as a result of drought or other climatic hazards, soil erosion, plant disease or insect attack have caused great hardship in some areas.

The Irish potato famine of 1845 is a notable historical example. This catastrophe led directly to the emigration of thousands from Ireland to Britain, the United States, Canada and Australia. Crop failure is still a danger facing the inhabitants of many developing countries, e.g. India. The continued occupation of areas liable to experience these hazards might suggest an indifference to the dangers of death, starvation or famine but out-migration from such areas may be based upon a recognition of the unattractiveness of these possibilities.

Push can also occur as a result of economic changes in rural villages. At one time many rural settlements possessed small industries, e.g. grain mills or small iron forges. During the Industrial Revolution factories in towns and cities

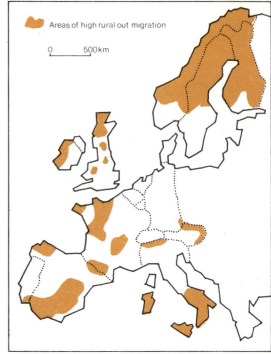

Fig. 6:8 *The principal areas suffering out-migration in Europe.*

expanded. Eventually many small firms in villages were unable to compete and had to close. The larger factories could benefit from economies of scale and from specializing in producing large amounts of particular products. Both trends meant their goods were cheaper than those from small local firms. They could also afford specialized machinery which was essential as products were developed. Reliability and consistency were difficult to maintain in small firms using very simple techniques.

People also leave rural areas because of the problems related to standards of service provision and of housing. As people move out of rural areas the whole community may ultimately be threatened. Others leave to follow friends and relatives and eventually too few remain to justify a primary school or a local shop.

A recent survey in Gloucestershire found that the following factors were the main reasons for people leaving agricultural employment:
1. Low pay
2. Long and uncertain hours of work
3. Failing health due to arduous work
4. Redundancy
5. Insecurity of employment
6. Poor working conditions.

In addition many labourers live in tied cottages. These houses are owned by the farmer. If the labourer loses his job, it also means the loss of the house. This situation also contributes to rural push in search of more security of housing tenure.

Apart from farming, other activities occur in rural areas, e.g. small cottage industries, fishing and mining or quarrying. The collapse of these activities can lead to the complete abandonment of a settlement. This is especially common in the case of mining when the resources become depleted, exhausted or unprofitable, e.g. the abandoning of tin mining settlements in Cornwall or gold mining settlements in California and Alaska.

Assignment

3   Fig. 6:9 illustrates the typical age/sex distribution of population in a rural community which is suffering from depopulation. Fig. 6:10 illustrates the pyramid for an expanding dormitory settlement. List the differences between the two pyramids. Why do you think there are comparatively few people in the fifteen to forty-five age groups in the settlements experiencing depopulation? Why is that group so large in Figure 6:10?

Urban pull factors such as employment opportunities, higher wages and better standards of facilities (and a much wider range of facilities) provide the magnetic attraction in the push-pull equation. As we saw in Chapter 5, urban areas also have problems. Some migrants from rural areas may only slightly improve their lot. It is the expectation of betterment that initiates migration, not a guarantee of success.

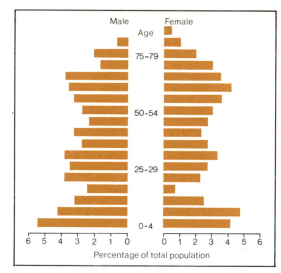

Fig. 6:9 *The Age-Sex pyramid of an area experiencing depopulation such as parts of the Highlands of Scotland.*

Stable or Developing Rural Settlement

Not all rural settlements are declining. Many service centres have reached a state of relative stability in terms of size of population. Other types of settlement are growing. Earlier we mentioned villages which were developing because of an influx of commuters. Some settlements in more remote locations have gained a tourist function in recent years. This has helped to reduce or even reverse the depopulation of the settlements because of the new opportunities for employment in facilities associated with tourism, e.g. shops, hotels, caravan parks and service trades. Farmers may supplement their income by offering bed and breakfast to tourists. Some residents may object to the changes and to the invasion by outsiders disrupting community life and values. The conflict often comes to the surface in the form of opposition to particular proposals for new developments such as the creation of a caravan park. Objections in terms of noise, pollution and spoiling the local environment illustrate the reaction to the changes and the feeling that the area and the community are threatened by such changes.

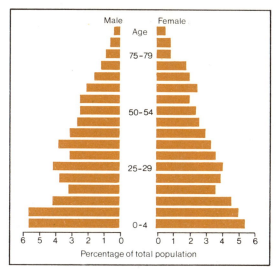

Fig. 6:10 *The Age-Sex pyramid of a growing suburban settlement or metropolitan village.*

Planners may seek to stabilize the population of an area by introducing small industries and other projects in a direct attempt to stem the drift of people from rural areas.

PROVISION OF SERVICES

If services are supplied on a commercial basis, then threshold requirements apply as they would in any urban situation. Even densely populated rural areas face problems in the provision of higher order goods. Sufficient people may not be willing to travel to a major centre to ensure the necessary threshold population for that good or service. Willingness to travel to a town for higher order services is affected by factors such as time and cost of travel and by the availability of transport. The reduction of bus services in rural areas may mean that people can only go to town on market days or on Saturdays. Even then it may mean catching the only bus so there is no flexibility about the timing of the trip. The removal or reduction of rural rail services has a similar effect. We can suggest, therefore, that willingness to travel will be a function of transport availability. It follows that the level of car ownership will provide a quick guide to this situation.

Another aspect of this topic is the trend in Britain and other developed countries toward larger shop units, e.g. supermarkets. These require a higher threshold than smaller shops. They do offer the probability of lower prices and a wider range of goods and provided transport is available this will lead to the closure of local shops in small villages.

In very different economic situations the factors affecting the provision of rural services will change in relative importance. For example, in rural India the people have a lower income than those in rural Britain. This affects the demand for goods. The range is also influenced by their inability to travel long distances because of the limited transport facilities and the cost of travel in relation to income. The level of services provided may therefore be simpler than those at centres of corresponding size in Britain.

Not all services in Britain are provided on a strictly commercial basis. Medical and educational services and various local and national government services are considered essential for the welfare of society. Thus we try to ensure that everyone has access to these facilities wherever possible. Nevertheless, the supply of these services is normally constrained by considerations of cost. It may not be possible to have a doctor in every village. One practice may serve a number of villages in addition to many farms. Local or national government services such as Registrars of Births, Deaths and Marriages, public health offices or rates and rents offices will also be centralized in most instances. Frequently the network of roads will favour the centralization of all these services into the same settlement because it is most favourably positioned to serve the local rural area. Sometimes the services are in different settlements either by accident of history or deliberate planning.

Many rural services perform a community function in addition to their direct commercial purpose. Figure 6:11 shows a butcher's shop in the market town of Moffat. Notice the signs advertising local community events. Similarly, inns and hotels often become the centre of community activities and the meeting place of groups, e.g. Young Farmer's Clubs.

Where the total population is so small or dispersed that permanent facilities are not possible, mobile shops are the principal source of service provision. Apart from grocery vans and other food suppliers, two other forms are important. First the provision of banking and library services. Second, experiments are taking place with alternative forms of service provision in these situations such as the post vans. These serve as mail carriers, rural buses, and also to deliver supplies to shops and houses.

In Britain, the elderly and the sick can be particularly disadvantaged in rural situations because of the problems of service provision. This can be especially acute in winter because of the additional climatic hazards of snow, ice or flooding.

What facilities should be supplied in order to sustain a rural community? The Devonshire County Plan (1964) suggested the pattern listed in Fig. 6:12.

This provides guide lines for the future location of facilities, but it does not necessarily describe the actual situation in that region. We can gain an insight into actual patterns from a study of Cambridgeshire villages (see Fig. 6:13).

The results may reflect the nature of the study area. Cambridgeshire has a fairly flat terrain and this may affect the spacing of settlements and the

Fig. 6:11 Shops in market towns often act as information points about clubs, associations, and local meetings.

hierarchy of centres. This pattern of service provision might not occur in areas with a different physical background, e.g. the Highlands and Islands of Scotland, highland Central Wales or the outback of Central and Western Australia. In the Outer Hebrides for example, there are difficulties relating to the supply of goods to shops. Ferry services can be disrupted by weather conditions, industrial strife or mechanical failure. In addition, the cost of transport adds to the price of the goods. These factors can favour a reduction in the total number of shops. Where the total population is small, one shop may have a monopoly of the provision of goods for a village or an island. These problems are shared by all remote or isolated small communities.

Public Utilities	Mains water; electricity; sewage
Social Facilities	Primary school; place of worship; village hall
Retail Facilities	Shops for day to day needs (grocery and newsagent); post office
Employment	This should be obtainable within the village or available nearby

Fig. 6:12 *Recommended facilities for a thriving rural community (Devon County Plan 1964).*

Fig. 6:13 *Facilities in villages in Cambridgeshire (County Development Plan 1968).*

Number of Inhabitants	Facilities
170-600	Public house, post office, hall and general store
600-1100	Also a primary school, playing field and a garage
1100-1800	Also a police house, butcher, ladies hairdresser and a doctor
1800-3000	Also an electrical goods shop, licensed grocer, hardware store and banks
3000 +	Also a secondary school and a chemist

Again few settlements in rural India or rural Nigeria would possess the variety of functions suggested by the Devonshire Plan. Most would certainly lack schools, doctors' surgeries and similar services. Periodic markets are very common in such areas and many villages with quite substantial populations often have no Central Place functions whatsoever. In these cases, service provision is closely related to the level of economic development and to elements of the traditional and cultural backgrounds of the areas as well as their physical environments.

Even in countries with similar levels of economic development the threshold population required for a particular service may vary, e.g. the minimum number of people for a primary school. This service is not determined solely on economic factors. We can calculate a figure on the basis of costs and teacher/pupil ratios but it is perfectly reasonable to argue that other criteria are more important. Opponents of the closure of local primary schools would stress the effect of such actions on the community and on the education of the children. Many people would argue that it is undesirable that young children should spend several hours each day travelling to school. Equally many would oppose the enforced separation of families which can occur when children from island and remote rural areas start secondary education. Daily travel is impossible and they have to live in hostels or lodgings. The provision of services is therefore a complex and sometimes controversial topic.

Assignment

4 Select a rural area of approximately 25 sq. km. From fieldwork and sources such as *Yellow Pages* and planning departments, plot the pattern of service provision. You should include information about mobile shops and post vans, if this is appropriate.

Write brief notes describing the pattern. When you explain the pattern you should refer to factors such as accessibility, planning and the functions of the different settlements in your study area.

Changing the Process of Depopulation

Before considering the measures needed to stop or even reverse the depopulation of rural areas we should consider the desirability or necessity of such actions. Some would argue that we should not interfere with natural processes. Others would oppose change because it might threaten the countryside and areas of natural beauty. An argument in favour of action is that many people would be happy to remain in rural areas if there were better employment prospects or better facilities. It can also be argued that man should try to make the best use of resources and rural areas are a potential resource. We should therefore try to make the best use of the land and physical and human resources of these areas. A possible additional benefit might occur if rural areas attracted people from urban settlements. This would help to reduce the pressures upon urban facilities such as housing. It might even lead to an improvement in standards of health because levels of pollution are normally much lower in rural areas.

Stopping, preventing and reversing the trend involves a very highly organized system of planned, co-ordinated action on the part of various people, particularly central and local government authorities. These bodies have to initiate plans designed to encourage population stability in the first instance and gradually work towards population growth. These plans involve employing one or more of the following measures either singly or in combination, depending on local circumstances.

First, steps can be taken to introduce some form of small-scale industry into rural settlements in order to widen employment opportunities. These industries may include textiles, crafts or tourism. Alternatively, large-scale projects employing large numbers of workers may be introduced into suitable areas, e.g. oil terminals, aluminium smelters and nuclear power stations. The net effect of these efforts would be to stop workers moving to city areas for employment and perhaps to attract people into these rural areas. In the Highlands of Scotland for example, several industrial growth points have been established in recent years through various agencies such as the Highlands and Islands Development Board, the Scottish Office and the Scottish Tourist Board. These included the paper mill at Corpach near Fort William, the aluminium smelter at Invergordon, the nuclear power station at Dounreay and the all-year tourist resort at Aviemore in the Cairngorms. Several thousand jobs were created through these projects which provided employment for both local people and for newcomers from other parts of Scotland a England.

Second, attempts can be made to improve communications and transport facilities in rural areas. This often involves making new road and rail links as well as improving existing networks. A great deal of public expenditure is required and governments invariably have to provide at least some of the finance. Governments must assess the importance of these projects compared to other demands for financial assistance. If these measures are undertaken, they often have an important impact on the efforts made to introduce new industry into rural areas. Accessibility is often a crucial consideration in industrial location involving factors such as mobility of labour, the supply of raw materials to the industries concerned and the distribution of finished products to markets. Improved communications may attract new industries and stimulate economic and population growth. Improved communications can also ease the problems of consumers living in rural areas and make it easier for them to reach a reasonable variety of services. This in turn may prevent their moving to towns and cities. However, as we have seen, increased mobility in this sense can sometimes have a bad effect on retail and other services already operating in rural settlements.

Third, a general improvement in the service provision of settlements in terms of shops, services, transport facilities, public utilities and medical services could stabilize population trends. But the provision of new shops and other service facilities depends greatly on existing threshold levels. If there are not sufficient people to support new functions, then it is not surprising that very few new establishments would be attracted in the hope that population might increase. Again, if transport facilities improve, more centres can compete for the trade of the consumers and this could weaken existing services in small villages. Population growth really has to be guaranteed before new retail provision can be made. Other services such as electricity, gas or water require an above average cost of provision and these extra costs may have to be borne by other consumers.

Fourth, measures can be adopted so as to rationalize the settlement pattern. This involves discouraging smaller settlement units in favour of larger ones. This has been tried in many Communist countries particularly the U.S.S.R. and Hungary. These efforts have been closely linked to the process of agricultural collectivization, i.e. the development of collective farming. In Hungary small settlements of under 300 persons have been run down whereas larger settlements in excess of 1500 have been strengthened by the addition of more service functions. The process of eliminating smaller settlements from rural areas has been much easier to implement in Communist countries than in Western countries with more democratic governments. Planners have made proposals for rationalization of settlement patterns in rural areas. For example, proposals were made to abandon declining mining villages in County Durham in an attempt to rationalize the settlement pattern. The planners could argue that the aim of the scheme would be to ensure an adequate level of service provision in all villages. Since small declining villages could not meet this level of provision, their inhabitants would benefit from the planned rationalization. The proposals met with fierce opposition and were finally rejected. In effect, the goals of the planners did not agree with goals (wishes) of the people. It should be noted that there is a widespread pattern of towns in Durham so that most inhabitants of declining mining villages were within reasonable travelling distance of the shopping facilities of a town. These conditions are relevant to a balanced understanding of the situation.

An example of the rationalization of rural settlement in Western Europe can be found in Holland. In the late 1940s rural settlements were planned for the North-East Polder which were based upon village regions of 4000 hectares, each region containing 3000 people and each village half that number. The village regions failed to attract the expected number of people and a later plan for a larger polder in East Flevoland increased the area of village regions to 9000 hectares and a planned total of 5000 people. At first twelve villages were planned but later the figure was reduced to fewer larger settlements each with a greater variety of functions. This plan proved more successful in the sense that the expected population was attained. The pattern of rationalization is shown in Fig. 6:14. The Dutch example may not be an indicator of general trends because it relates to the development of the pattern in a new agricultural area. Many governments wish to rationalize rural patterns but they must overcome the reluctance of people to move from their traditional home to other enlarged villages. In 1952, India introduced a programme of rural rationalization based upon more than fifty project areas. Each project area contained many villages. Some rationalization of the pattern has occurred aided by the fact that the larger villages have become centres for agricultural and medical advisory services but the rate of change is comparatively slow. People retain strong bonds of attachment to their plots, their houses and their village.

Stopping, preventing or reversing rural depopulation depends upon the implementation of a wide variety of programmes designed to improve the attractiveness of living in rural settlements. Yet, despite these measures, depopulation continues in many rural areas. This may suggest that, where mobility is unrestricted by governments or other controls, depopulation is difficult to combat. It may also mean that we are using the wrong approach to the problem or that the scale of investment in programmes designed to combat depopulation is too small to produce more than localized success. The problem is very complex because of the many factors which can influence the decision to move away from a rural area. The failure of new industries which use the natural resources of the area, e.g. pulp making, is certainly very disappointing and does suggest that many of the problems as yet remain unsolved.

Fig. 6:14 *Changes in settlement patterns in Dutch polders (after H. CLOUT). Notice that the distances between the villages in East Flevoland Polder are greater than those in the North-east Polder. Service areas would also be correspondingly larger.*

Fig. 6:15 *Soil erosion at a tourist honeypot caused by visitors wearing a path on a hillside.*

Tourism and Rural Areas

Throughout Britain and Europe there are many areas of natural scenic beauty including for example the Central Highlands of Scotland, Snowdonia, the Lake District, the moorlands of Dartmoor and Exmoor, the Bavarian Foreland and the Puy de Dôme in the Massif Central. Added to these are numerous coastal areas in which settlements have an immediate appeal for the holiday tourist trade. Many thousands visit these areas and this can create many problems. One of the most urgent problems is that of ensuring that the rural environment is protected from the less desirable effects of tourism. These effects include heavy congestion on roads in rural areas, pollution from litter, dumping and traffic fumes, fire damage, damage to property, plants and wildlife, the unplanned development of car parks and caravan sites and the erosion of land through overuse as illustrated in Fig. 6:15. These prob-

lems have long been recognized by local and central governments and great efforts have been made in a variety of ways to overcome them. One solution is to set aside large areas of protected countryside such as National Parks.

Planning measures can be introduced to control the location, function and style of new buildings. Old buildings of cultural or historic interest are often protected by preservation orders and by the work of bodies such as the National Trust. Their efforts are vital since they are protecting our national heritage. Fig. 6:18 illustrates this kind of protected building. A great deal of money is often required for the upkeep or restoration of these properties. Some comes from grants made by central government but a large proportion is obtained from gifts from the public. Entrance charges also help to finance the maintenance of these buildings. Tourists are an important source of entrance money but the provision of bus parks, car parks and toilet facilities may fall as a burden upon the local authority of the particular rural

district. This money may have to be found by increasing local rates. Planners may therefore insist that the facilities are provided by the owners of the houses before agreeing that the premises be opened to the public.

In general, tourists create demands for facilities. Problems can result for communities ranging from the supply of parking spaces to the provision of adequate roads. Tourism may not justify new shops nor the local authorities creating additional facilities because of the scale and nature of the demands. During the off-peak season, in bad weather or periods of economic recession, specially provided facilities would be unused. On a few days at the peak of the season the available facilities may be completely inadequate for the maximum demand, Shops, for example, could not exist simply on the demand which occurs on less then ten days in a year. Some balance must be reached in decision-making by shopkeepers, other businesses and local authorities which involves a realistic assessment of demand.

Within major tourist regions, settlements sited on major routes can sustain specialist facilities for tourists, e.g. knitwear shops, crafts, souvenirs, antiques, cafés and hotels. 'Honeypot' locations, places which attract large volumes of tourists such as the Trossachs in Scotland, the Lake and Peak Districts, Snowdonia, the Cotswolds and Dartmoor satisfy the conditions required to justify the economic arguments for providing special facilities. Settlements such as Aberfoyle and Callander at the edge of the Trossachs or Bakewell in the Peak District are excellent examples of these settlements.

Assignment

5 A possible field project which you could undertake would be to compare a settlement of the type described above during off-season and the peak season. Compile lists of the facilities provided in each season. A comparison of the lists will give you an indication of the facilities which are dependent upon tourism. You could also count the number of different types of vehicles in the car parks on each occasion. Comment on the differences.

Second Homes

The term **second home** covers a wide variety of dwellings including caravans, converted cottages, architect-designed villas and chalets and even houseboats. These buildings may be found in clusters or they may be dispersed over a wide area. Prior to 1945, second homes in Britain were generally limited to a very small section of society. In the post-war period, more and more people have been able to devote a larger share of their income to buying or renting second homes in rural or coastal areas. If they live in city areas, the homes provide a means of escape during the holiday or week-end periods to the relative peace and quiet of the countryside.

Improved access to countryside areas has greatly helped in the growth of this phenomenon. In 1970 teachers at Wye College estimated that a total of 180-200 000 second homes (excluding caravans and houseboats) were scattered throughout non-urban areas of England and Wales. They forecast that by 1985 this figure would be as high as 600-700 000, and possibly rise to two million by 2000 A.D.

Figures for European countries show that second homes are increasing. In some countries this increase has been quite dramatic. For example, in France the number rose from 447 000 in 1954 to an estimated 1.6 million in 1971. In Sweden the number of recorded second homes in 1969 was nearly half a million. By 1979 this had risen to almost one million.

Many of these homes have been built at or near coastal sites in rural areas. The distance travelled from primary residences, that is houses where owners have their permanent homes, varies from about 70 kilometres in Europe, to over 350 kilometres in the United States. It is quite common for people to accept distances of up to 250 kilometres as being reasonable for a week-end trip. Car ownership and the quality of roads obviously affect the distance factor.

The effects of this pattern on seasonal suburbanization of the countryside are twofold. First, rural areas often derive certain advantages from having a large number of second homes. These include the restoration of obsolete farms and the building of new residences. Land which is of little agricultural value might prove attractive as sites for second-home development. Local farmers can profit from the sale of land for these developments. Rural authorities may gain additional income from rates. Businesses such as shops, cafés, garages and small builders all benefit from the increased demand for their services. There can also be disadvantages for the rural areas. Agricultural land is invaded and it may not necessarily be poor land. This can lead to a loss of agricultural production. The new houses cause a visible change in the local environment which often angers landscape conservationists. Great emphasis is therefore placed on the need for developments to harmonize with local landscapes and buildings in terms of style and location. Caravans need to be screened from view in an attempt to blend the development into the landscape. Farmers and more especially agricultural labourers often find themselves unable to compete financially with second-home owners for the available housing. Despite the construction of new houses and renovations of old cottages, there can still be a shortage of adequate housing for permanent local residents.

Conflict can develop between the locals and second-home owners. An issue can trigger strong feelings. For example, a rise in rates because local authorities are forced to lay new water and sewage pipes to service the second homes is a common cause of dissent between the two groups within the rural areas. Some argue that many attractive areas of countryside are in danger of being saturated by second homes. Certainly the character of many rural communities is changing. The cottages house architects and advertising executives, the water storage tanks are replaced with swimming pools. Attitudes to such changes will inevitably vary. One unsolved question is how we could measure saturation in this sense. Can you suggest some suitable criteria? Perhaps we could refer to the number of houses, or the percentage of houses owned as second homes.

National Parks

Throughout England and Wales, Europe and North America and other parts of the world many large tracts of rural land have been designated as National Parkland. A report called the Dower Report published in 1945 defined a British national park as follows: 'Each National Park should comprise an extensive area of beautiful and relatively wild country in which for the nation's benefit and by appropriate national decision and action, the following should obtain:

1. Characteristic landscape beauty strictly preserved
2. Access and facilities for public open-air enjoyment amply provided
3. Wildlife and buildings and places of architectural and historic interest suitably protected
4. Established farming use effectively maintained.'

It was suggested that since these parks were intended for the good of the nation, their financial costs should be met by the central government, from government funds. However, the parks were eventually financed partly from government funds and partly from the rate funds of local

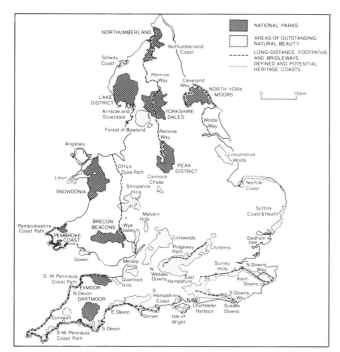

Fig. 6:16 National Parks and areas of outstanding beauty in England and Wales.

WATER CATCHMENT Several valleys have been flooded to provide reservoirs to meet the demands for water supply for local urban areas.

FARMING Mainly sheep farming, (farmers are not discouraged from ploughing up and fencing areas of "high visual amenity").

FORESTRY Conifers are displacing deciduous woodland areas.

7

1

DARTMOOR NATIONAL PARK

Total area 950 sq.km

Moorland 500 sq.km

Woodland and cultivated land 450 sq.km

INDUSTRIAL LAND USE Mining for china clay (Kaolin). Quarrying of igneous rock and recent testing for geothermal power potential.

2

MILITARY TRAININGS CAMPS These use 11·3% of the land area of the park for training and artillery ranges. All sites are restricted.

6

HOUSING DEVELOPMENT Increase in the number of second holiday homes. Increase in number of commuters. Steady increase in demand from retired persons for homes.

3

COMMUNICATIONS Access roads (to cope with great increase in number of cars). Nature trails and paths. Electricity pyions. Radio and television masts.

5

4

DEMAND FOR ADDITIONAL HOLIDAY AND LEISURE FACILITIES Caravan and camping sites, (taking up to 30% of visitors residential in the area). Sports facilities. Picnic areas. Car parks.

Fig. 6:17 Pressures upon the use of land in Dartmoor National Park.

authorities into whose control the organization and administration of the parks passed. In this way the British parks were quite different from parks in the United States. The latter were and still are operated by a national body called the National Parks Service. In Britain a National Parks Commission was established in 1949 with the express purpose of preserving and enhancing the natural beauty of ten parkland areas in England and Wales (see Fig. 6:16). In addition to these tasks, the Commission also had to provide facilities for outdoor recreation for people visiting the parklands. The National Parks Commission was replaced by the Countryside Commission in 1968 by Act of Parliament. This new body had a much wider range of interest. In addition to the National Parks it was also involved with all matters pertaining to the provision and improvement of facilities for the enjoyment of the countryside. In addition to the parks, the new Commission was concerned with National Forest parkland and a variety of areas designated as areas of natural scenic beauty, e.g. Cannock Chase.

Apart from financial difficulties, the National Parks have faced many other problems, not the least of which has been coping with tremendous pressure on land use. Fig. 6:17 shows the competition for land in Dartmoor National Park.

Other difficulties included pressure caused by the huge increase in the numbers of people visiting the parklands. Exmoor Park Committee estimated that because of road improvements the number of people living within a three-and-a-half-hour journey from the park increased from 5 million to 19 million during the period 1970 to 1980.

Another problem which visitors to the parks have encountered is one of access. Access within the parks is not unrestricted. Areas of enclosed land and privately owned estates are protected from trespassers. Here again the parks differ from American parklands.

Today, in addition to the ten National Parks in England and Wales, there are also eight parks designated as National Forest Parks plus several areas called areas of outstanding beauty. In order to preserve the landscape within the parks, severe restrictions have been imposed on housing developments in terms of the number and style; on industrial development and on similar types of land use. Wildlife is protected as are various species of plants and trees. People visiting the parks are encouraged in a wide variety of recreational pursuits including sailing and water skiing on, for example, Lakes Windermere, Ullswater and Coniston in the Lake district, pot-holing and caving in the Peak District and climbing in Snowdonia. Facilities include nature trails, viewpoints, hostels, car parks, access points, rest

111

huts and information centres. In some areas, however, problems of pollution and soil erosion caused by visitors to the parks often result in parts of the parks being fenced off from the tourists. The dual aims of the Countryside Commission of preservation whilst attracting visitors, may seem almost contradictory. Certainly conflict can arise over the attainment of both aims.

Although there are National Parks in England and Wales, there are none in Scotland. This is due partly to the fact that in Scotland access to open country has always been relatively easier than in England and Wales. Moreover, in terms of land use, population pressures have always been much less in Scotland because there is a much larger proportion of countryside. Although there are no National Parks, there are Forest Parks which have been created by the Forestry Commission in the belief that where land was acquired for the planting of new forests, it should remain open for public enjoyment.

In order to protect many villages which because of their distinctive and architectural interest add something to the general scenic value of rural areas, many local government restrictions on land-use development now operate. Many villages have been declared Conservation Areas and all modern buildings must be designed so as to blend into the existing character of the area in which they are built.

Fig. 6:18 shows the location of the main forest parks and areas of outstanding scenic attraction where facilities are provided for visitors. These facilities include accommodation such as hotels and hostels, information centres, entertainment amenities and rest lodges such as the one at Glencoe, which is provided and maintained by the National Trust for Scotland.

National Parklands are also common in Europe. Sweden for example has sixteen National Parks, the earliest of which (Abisoo, Sarek, Peljakaise, Sonfsallet, Halra and Angso) were established in 1909. These parks were designed to: 'provide scientists of today and tomorrow with virgin country for their researches and to give people

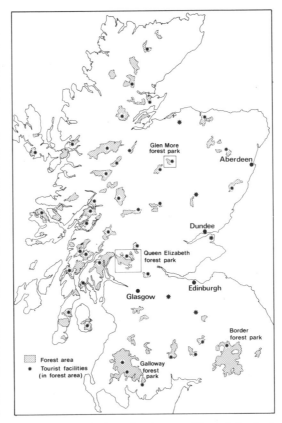

Fig. 6:18 Forest Parks, and major areas of forest, in Scotland.

opportunities of recreation in wild country, hiking country and cultivated regions . . .' (Swedish Forestry Service.)

The size and accessibility of the parks vary widely. The smallest are Halra and Angso — 27 hectares, and the largest is Paldselang — 204 000 hectares.

In France, especially in the Massif Central region, National Parks provide the city populations with 'lungs' away from the polluted industrialized urban areas. Parks in the Massif Central include a wide variety of scenery with old volcanic cones, calderas and sills, remnants of an old volcanic zone in the Puy de Dôme. These northern parts of the Massif contrast with the limestone areas further south in the Cevennes and Causses

areas. Other parklands in France are located in the south-east near the French Alps and to the north-east near the German border. All serve the basic function of land and scenic conservation.

As we said earlier, the National Parks in the U.S.A. are quite different from those in Britain. Officially they are defined as: 'A relatively large area, distinguished by the scientific importance of its wildlife or beauty of its scenery and occupied by one or more ecosystems which have been little affected by human exploitation and occupation . . . If visitors are allowed to enter such areas, they must do so under special conditions.'

In effect entry to the parks is controlled by an official government body called the National Park Service. This body administers several different types of parklands, national monuments and places and buildings of historic and cultural interest. There are 320 such places in all, of which only thirty-seven are designated as National Parks. The parklands are listed and shown in Figs. 6:19 and 6:20. The National Park Service looks after land areas totalling some 77 million acres throughout the United States, ranging from small tracts of land such as National Battlefields to large areas such as Parkways, Lakeshore and Seashore as well as the National Parks.

American National Parks offer a wide range of recreational facilities, e.g. camping and boating. Many require visitors to pay an entrance fee. The preserved environments include the historical battlefields, historic buildings and Indian tribal lands. One strange example is the former federal prison on Alcatraz Island in San Francisco Bay. In essence the parks signify the attempts to conserve the scenic, historical and cultural heritage of the U.S.A.

An interesting development is the creation of National Recreation Areas. One such area in the middle of the megalopolis on the north-eastern seaboard of the United States (Gateway National Recreation Area) attracts 9 million visitors per year yet it only covers the equivalent of 1 per cent of the acreage of Yellowstone National Park (Figure 6:21). Not everyone agrees that particular districts should be set aside as National Parks.

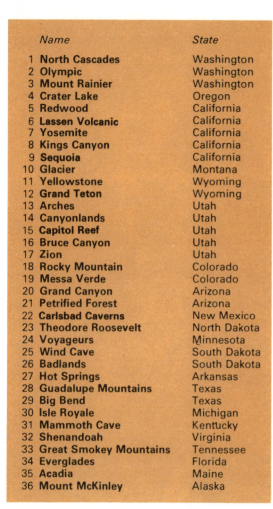

Name	State
1 North Cascades	Washington
2 Olympic	Washington
3 Mount Rainier	Washington
4 Crater Lake	Oregon
5 Redwood	California
6 Lassen Volcanic	California
7 Yosemite	California
8 Kings Canyon	California
9 Sequoia	California
10 Glacier	Montana
11 Yellowstone	Wyoming
12 Grand Teton	Wyoming
13 Arches	Utah
14 Canyonlands	Utah
15 Capitol Reef	Utah
16 Bruce Canyon	Utah
17 Zion	Utah
18 Rocky Mountain	Colorado
19 Messa Verde	Colorado
20 Grand Canyon	Arizona
21 Petrified Forest	Arizona
22 Carlsbad Caverns	New Mexico
23 Theodore Roosevelt	North Dakota
24 Voyageurs	Minnesota
25 Wind Cave	South Dakota
26 Badlands	South Dakota
27 Hot Springs	Arkansas
28 Guadalupe Mountains	Texas
29 Big Bend	Texas
30 Isle Royale	Michigan
31 Mammoth Cave	Kentucky
32 Shenandoah	Virginia
33 Great Smokey Mountains	Tennessee
34 Everglades	Florida
35 Acadia	Maine
36 Mount McKinley	Alaska

Fig. 6:19 The National Parks of mainland U.S.A.

For example, in Alaska there is a conflict of interests between conservationists seeking to preserve the wilderness and developers wanting access to oil and other important natural resources. It is not always easy to reconcile these conflicting interests or decide which is most important in the short term and the long term for both local inhabitants and national interests. Indeed, there may be differences of opinion between local residents and non-local pressure groups.

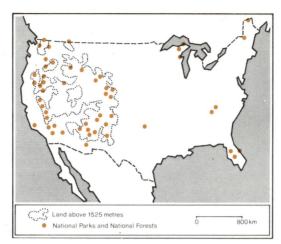

Fig. 6:20 The distribution of American National Parks and some of the major National Forests.

Metropolitan Villages

Some rural settlements have become an extension of the city set in the country. The term **Metropolitan Village** has been coined to describe the situation and the processes of colonization by urban dwellers. A planning study in South Merseyside found that many metropolitan villages had a majority of their residents engaged in what are termed professional occupations (lawyers, managers, bankers, teachers, accountants, salesmen). Members of this group have both physical and economic mobility in that they own cars and can afford the cost of commuting.

The colonization of these villages leads to social and economic changes. The level of services increases to meet the new demand. Apart from changes in land use, there are significant changes in the size and structure of population. These changes can be documented by making reference to either national census information such as the 1961, 1971 and 1981 Census, or Valuation Rolls over the same period. The Merseyside study concluded that when a metropolitan village reaches a population of 7000 it has left village status and is now a small town. But does it resemble a settlement such as Malton (see Chapter 2) in terms of functions and services? You will recall that Mal-

Fig. 6:21 Gateway National Recreation Area (after National Geographic Society).

ton is a market town with an extensive variety of Central Place functions and some local industry. Metropolitan villages on the other hand are perhaps closer to being extra large dormitory settlements tied by commuting to the nearby city. The village of Killearn in what used to be West Stirlingshire (now Central Region) is another typical example.

Case Study 1—Killearn (Fig. 6:22)

Throughout the period 1831 to 1960, this settlement was typically rural. Located some 25 kilometres from the nearest urban settlement, Glasgow, most of the inhabitants of Killearn were employed in some form of agricultural activity. During the 1960s and particularly the 1970s the character of the settlement began to change quite markedly with the construction of new private housing estates. These were built mainly along the edge of the two main roads, Glasgow and

Station Roads. The structure of the village was visibly altered from a linear pattern to one more amorphous in character. The population increased from about 200 to around 2800 (1980). This was accompanied by a similar expansion in the number and range of service facilities. These now include two mini-markets, a sub-post office, a hairdresser, an hotel, a public house, a bank, a primary school and a new clinic. In addition to these, several mobile shops visit the village and the housing estates. Few residents work in the local area. Over 400 cars go into the Glasgow area, a measure of commuting to work. Further journeys are made at week-ends for weekly shopping although the town of Stirling (32 kilometres) also attracts many shoppers from the village. Any houses for sale in the village are almost exclusively advertised in Glasgow daily newspapers and their sales are handled by estate agents from the city, thus strengthening the links between the two settlements. Despite the distance between Glasgow and Killearn, some 25 kilometres, this village is definitely within the rural-urban fringe area of Glasgow and has become a commuter suburb of the city.

Problems are eventually caused by continual growth in these metropolitan villages. The sewage system or the local school may be unable to cope with the additional strain imposed on them by increased housing development. Facilities must be extended, e.g. temporary classrooms or alternatively, new housing must be stopped. In essence, the metropolitan village suffers from the opposite set of problems facing areas of depopulation. In this case, schools face overcrowding and other facilities experience excessive demands. As we mentioned in Chapter 5, some metropolitan planners now believe that further expansion of these villages should stop with future growth being channelled into the redeveloped inner zones of the cities. The solution is logical and even desirable. It is questionable, however, if it is a policy which will find support from the people who want to move to metro-

politan villages and who find their aspirations blocked by planning committees. This is another example of the potential conflict of interests which confront those attempting to plan and control the changing pattern of rural settlement. The changes result from different factors, and planning policies must reflect the various situations. They must also contain a considerable measure of flexibility to accommodate future changes in particular circumstances such as falling birth rates in Britain, or perhaps a technological revolution resulting from the development of microprocessors. The latter may result in increased redundancy in industry which in turn could have an effect on the demand for housing in metropolitan villages. A ranking of priorities must emerge such as those proposed by Devon County Council in relation to the facilities required for a thriving rural community.

Assignments

6   Make a list of your planning priorities for:
(a)   An area of depopulation
(b)   A metropolitan village.
For either (a) or (b) try to explain why you consider your particular priorities to be important. Show how by adopting your policies you can overcome the problems which these settlements face.

Perhaps your class can arrange themselves into opposing groups representing different sections of the community, e.g. local residents, new residents, local authorities and town planners. Each group can suggest and support arguments for their own proposals for future development in the settlement.

7   Carry out a study, similar to that on Killearn, for a village near which (or in which) you live. How far is it from its nearest urban centre? Chart its population (from Census data) at ten-yearly intervals: When did it being to change its character? What new services did it acquire and when? Use a large-scale O.S. map to show the original village and the new built-up areas. Calculate the proportion of the inhabitants engaged in rural occupations before and after the village changed its character.

Revision Questions

1   What do you understand by the following terms: rural settlement; linear form; settlement nucleation; dispersed distribution.
2   List the main factors which contribute to
(a)   Nucleated (agglomerated) patterns
(b)   Dispersed patterns
of settlement distribution.
3   What is rural depopulation? Why does it happen? Refer to examples.
4   What steps have been taken to prevent and reverse the depopulation of rural areas?
5   What are the main effects of depopulation in rural communities?
6   How are countryside areas in danger of becoming semi-urbanized? How have second homes contributed to this problem?
7   List the chief effects of tourism on rural areas and settlements.
8   How are the following affected by tourism in rural areas:
(a)   Accessibility
(b)   Service provision
(c)   Land conservation programmes?
9   What are National Parks? How do British parks differ from those in the United States? Refer to: size; distribution; types; organization.
10   Discuss the chief types of land-use conflict found within British National Parks.
11   How would you attempt to find out about changes which are occurring in rural areas in respect of:
(a)   Employment structure
(b)   Population patterns?
12   What are metropolitan villages? In your opinion are such settlements a desirable addition to rural areas? Explain your answer.

Fig. 6:22 Killearn.

CHAPTER SEVEN
FIELD STUDIES

Introduction

Fieldwork is an essential part of geographical studies. It can involve learning to recognize particular features and developing skills of describing and recording information about them. In this chapter we are mainly concerned with field projects. These require a clear statement of what features or relationships are to be studied and careful construction of the design of the project so as to ensure success. A simple method involves three stages:

1. State the topic, problem or relationship to be studied
2. Collect the information
3. Analyse the information and comment on the results.

We could, for example, state our topic as the study of a farm or village. We may want to achieve a comprehensive analysis of either phenomenon. However, stage 2 is simplified if we establish more specific targets. Thus, for a farm study, we may decide to investigate a series of relationships such as land use and altitude, land use and soil quality, land use and drainage, farm economy and distance from market and farm economy and agricultural subsidies. It is still possible to arrive at a fairly comprehensive picture of the farm but the collection of data stage is clarified because these specific topics have been identified. These topics can be stated as **hypotheses**. For example, we could suggest that the proportion of arable land would decrease with increasing altitude. It is possible to investigate the relationship and decide the degree of validity of this statement. The hypothesis might prove to be accurate in most parts of Britain but not in other regions of the world, e.g. the wet tropics. The construction of hypotheses or the identification of topics for investigation result primarily from our existing knowledge of relationships between different elements in the environment. Books, maps and photographs are all valuable aids which can be used at this stage. Once the topic has been identified it is normally prudent to study maps and photographs of the area and any other appropriate information which can be found in a library, e.g. census material relating to town population or the population of a region. Some relationships can be investigated on the basis of map and photographic evidence and then studied in greater detail in the field using other techniques such as questionnaires to gather more information.

Organization is an essential part of the successful project, particularly with reference to the collection and recording of information. You might think that we would want as much information as possible. Remember, however, that there is little value in gathering a mountain of facts unless you can organize and assemble them into a usable form. For example, it might seem obvious on a farm study to record everything relating to land use, soil quality, altitude and drainage characteristics for every field but it is only self-evident when hypotheses are stated and the study has specific aims which depend upon using data of this particular nature. Otherwise much of the information gathered may be unnecessary. Clearly, many relationships cannot be analysed without comprehensive data, e.g. information about all fields on a farm or every building in a village. In many cases an annotated fieldmap (a map of the area with detailed notes written on in the field survey about land use and other relevant characteristics) provides the basic source of recorded data. This should always be supplemented by a field notebook. The notebook must relate to the map so that the information can be located. Thus in a farm study fields may require to be numbered. The same numbering should be used in the notebook as on the map. The notebook can record details about land-use classification, include field sketches and notes and details of discussions, e.g. interviews with farmers.

The notebook means that an open-ended element can be introduced into the study because points can be readily recorded. Equally, it is important to establish the basic aims of the study before starting the fieldwork. The open-ended element means that you can adapt slightly and take advantage of a particular piece of information or react to a particular, unforeseen, situation.

Sometimes a questionnaire survey may be used. For example, we may question shoppers in an attempt to define the hinterland of a centre. The questions should be selected carefully and the respondents chosen by random sample. The technique is outlined in greater detail in Chapter 5, Gordon and Dick, *Urban Geography*. That chapter also describes various ways of analysing data, the third stage of the project. Briefly, the analysis can involve map or other pictorial techniques (graphs and histograms) and/or statistical calculations (averages, correlations). The remainder of this chapter will describe some fieldwork topics in settlement geography.

Farm Study

The information required will be determined by the topics to be studied but the following list summarizes the principal features:

1. Site of farm buildings
2. Site of fields
3. Relief, slope, aspect, drainage, soil and use of fields, amounts of fertilizer, livestock data
4. Farm buildings and machinery
5. Markets; location, frequency of use, prices, etc.
6. Sources of raw materials, amounts
7. Agricultural subsidies and other influences on farm economy
8. Use of fields each year for past three or five years
9. Any major changes in farm economy
   (a) which have occurred in the last decade
   (b) planned for immediate future
10. Farming year
11. Farm tenure (owned, rented, etc.)
12. Labour
13. Other details, e.g. field shapes, field walls, hedgerows, farm facilities (water, electricity, telephone, etc.) building materials and style, accessibility within farm and to markets.

Slope, for example, can be measured from maps or in the field using either an Abney Level or a clinometer (depending upon your familiarity with the use of these instruments). The map technique involves calculating the average gradient as given by the formula

$$\text{Average Gradient} = \frac{\text{Vertical Interval}}{\text{Horizontal Distance}}$$

and expressed as a ratio, e.g. 1 in 12 or 1 in 50. As you will probably know this means that for every 12 metres of horizontal distance the land rises on average by *one* metre. Slope can affect the land use and also the method of farming. For example, in many parts of the world, particularly South-East Asia and India, steep slopes are terraced so as to create areas of flat land and to prevent soil erosion. In Britain the angle of slope can inhibit the use of tractors and other farm machinery. We have stressed this particular example, slope, to illustrate the importance of measurement and the recording of detailed information relating to the geography of the farm under study.

The recording of land use requires a classification scheme. It is useful to adopt some standard scheme such as the one in the Second Land Utilization Survey of Britain (see Fig. 7:1). For a farm study you would specify different arable crops, e.g. barley, oats, turnips, potatoes, etc. It would be important to identify rough grazing as a separate category from unusable land.

Particular features may be important in certain farms, e.g. artificial drainage or the use of irrigation, and information should be collected about any topic which helps to explain the farm economy.

It is useful to conduct a comparative study of farming selecting different types of farms or farms in different situations or farms in apparently similar situations. The choice would depend upon the purpose of the study. Thus, if the relationship between altitude and land use is

Fig. 7:1 Categories of land use (adapted from Second land Utilisation Survey).

Major Classes	Sub-types
Arable Land	Cereals
	Ley Legumes, e.g. beans or peas
	Roots
	Green Fodder
	Industrial Crops
	Fallow
Market Gardening	Field Vegetables
	Mixed
	Nurseries
	Allotments
	Flowers
	Soft fruits
	Hops
Orchards	With Grass
	With Arable Land
	With Market Gardening
Grassland	(Permanent, Temporary)
Heath, Moorland, Roughland	
Water and Marsh	
Woodland	Various sub-types, coniferous, deciduous, etc.
Derelict	
Transport	Grades of Road
Building	Type, Materials, Age, Use

to be examined it would be important to span a range of heights in order to test the idea thoroughly.

Agricultural land use can also be studied by means of transects. Three transects each two kilometres wide and six kilometres in length can provide valuable information for comparative analysis. For example, hypotheses relating land use to altitude or slope or soil quality can be examined. A further possibility is the use of a sample survey. This is particularly appropriate if the purpose is to examine agricultural patterns in a region.

Village Study

The study will probably describe and examine the development and structure of the village. In addition to these general aims, specific relationships may be studied such as the relationship between land use and distance from the centre of the village or the main transport route. The study may also examine the relationship of the village to the surrounding agricultural area and to other settlements in the district. This introduces the study of hinterlands which we will consider later.

A detailed field study should include information relating to:

(a) Type of buildings, e.g. houses, shops, farms, etc.

(b) Size and style of buildings, e.g. number of storeys, detached, terraced, etc.

(c) Age of buildings (exact if possible, dates are sometimes on buildings, alternatively broad categories, nineteenth-century, pre-1939, post-1960, etc.)

(d) Location of buildings (these should be plotted on a plan and details about the site recorded in your notebook).

The age of buildings can provide useful clues to the pattern of growth of a village. This may be checked against any available old maps of the village. Population data can normally be obtained from local planning departments. These may indicate population trends, growth or decline. They are also important in studies of facilities and amenities in villages. A simple count of the various facilities, school, telephone kiosks, doctor's surgeries, police office, shops, etc., can become meaningful when the numbers of each facility are compared with the resident population. By studying a number of villages it may be possible to identify problems of service provision in particular villages.

An investigation of the social geography of the village might involve a questionnaire survey of residents supplemented by information about various community activities, e.g. youth groups, Women's Rural Institute, church membership, gala days, etc. For example, we might expect that the situation of a village would influence the social geography of the settlement. We would expect dormitory villages to differ from agricultural villages. How could we measure these differences?

One approach would involve a survey of buildings and facilities in the village. The dormitory village would have more houses of recent construction than the agricultural village and particularly more houses in private ownership. A questionnaire survey would supplement this information by providing answers on the location of workplace of the head of household. Questions about the involvement of the family in community activities might also show differences between newcomers and more established residents of the village. However, many studies have found that after a few years newcomers are not easily identified from more established residents in terms of community involvement. Differences do remain in terms of income. In a dormitory village for example, the commuters will have a higher level of car ownership than the locals.

Sphere of Influence Study

In Chapter 3 various methods of determining the sphere of influence were mentioned. Using a particular function as an indicator the study would proceed as follows:

1. Select the indicator function(s). Facilities which make deliveries to customers may be a ready source of data, e.g. butchers' shops or laundries (see Chapter 3).

2. Test this hinterland by comparison with the results of a questionnaire survey of shoppers using the shopping centre. This survey can either be conducted in the centre or at various points throughout the possible hinterland. Questions would include place of purchase of various goods and source of various services and may also seek information about frequency of visits to the centre and mode of transport (bus, car, etc.).

The above criteria relate to the shopping and service hinterlands of the settlement. Another sphere of influence will relate to the catchment area of industrial employees and the location of industrial raw materials and markets for manufactured goods. These can be investigated in a similar fashion to the method outlined above. In this case data about the firm would be obtained by interview with the owner or manager and information about the catchment area for labour by questioning employees and local residents.

It is often possible to identify an intensive portion of the sphere of influence of a settlement related to the journey-to-work zone and a larger more extensive sphere related only to certain shopping and service functions. Thus, the two approaches outlined could supply the information required for an investigation of this hypothesis.

When interviewing shopkeepers or industrialists, it is important to arrange a suitable appointment in advance and to take a map so that some accuracy can be introduced into the statements about hinterlands and excessive vagueness avoided. Always be pleasant, patient and polite. Equally, you will probably need to be persistent. Many people in commerce and industry are initially reluctant to part with even the tiniest scraps of information. It is a good idea to prepare a list of the points you want answered so that you are organized. Do not, however, confront a shopkeeper or industrialist with a massive questionnaire. The response is liable to be 'Goodbye!'

The same methodology applies if you are studying the catchment area of a particular facility, e.g. a sports centre. In this instance, a questionnaire survey of users is the obvious approach. However, you may also want to investigate why people do not use the facility. That part of the study would involve a sample survey of households

within the catchment area (defined from the user survey). You could suggest possible reasons, e.g. age, or availability of transport, which might affect the likelihood of particular types of people or people in particular situations using that facility. The questionnaire would have to include questions related to these points in addition to seeking other possible explanations. The latter may involve listing possible factors and asking respondents to indicate those which were relevant and to add other influential features not on the list.

If you interview in a town or city the selection of the location is important. An obvious choice would be near the principal variety or department stores. You will obtain some variation in the results depending upon the day and even the time of the day you carry out your survey. To study the maximum shopping hinterland, you should select a Saturday or in a market town, the market day. Whether the interviews are conducted at the shopping centre or on people's door steps, it is important to be brief. Remember to select the sample carefully. Avoid bias such as interviewing only males or only females or only people of one particular age group. In a shopping centre the simplest solution is to interview the Xth person (X being determined by the time available and the number of questionnaires to be completed). Similarly, in a household survey you would interview every Xth house. For example, if there were 1000 houses and you wanted to conduct 100 interviews X would equal 10. You would select every 10th house from a list of addresses such as the Voters Roll.

Figs. 7:2a and 7:2b, show the influence of two selected functions which are located in the town of Stirling. The sphere of influence for deliveries from the major store is very extensive because there are no branches in Edinburgh or Glasgow. A composite picture of the sphere of influence of Stirling is shown in Fig. 7:3.

We can see that the general boundary of the sphere of influence of Stirling extends north-west to Callander, west to Killearn and south-west to Kilsyth. The boundary marks the transition from the sphere of influence of one centre to that of another centre of equal or higher order. Thus the northern, eastern and south-eastern limits illustrate competition from Perth, Dunfermline and Falkirk respectively.

Hierarchy or Ranking Study

The purpose of the study is to investigate the orders of Central Places in the area. Using a list of functions such as that shown in Fig. 7:4, count the number of establishments of each functional type in each settlement. You might add other factors such as cinemas, banks, garage, doctor, dentist, solicitor, hotel and police station to give a more broadly-based range of activities. When functions of different levels occur then major orders of settlements can readily be identified. For example, a large town will have department stores and variety stores whereas a village will only have convenience shops and a limited number of other services. It is, however, difficult to recognize finer shadings without some system of weighting the relative importance of different functions. One method is to use a **centrality value** devised by W. K. Davies. For example, if there are 50 bakers in an area, the centrality value of

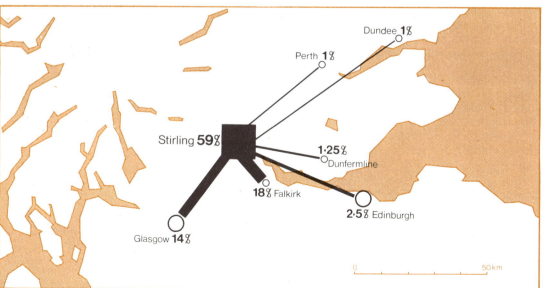

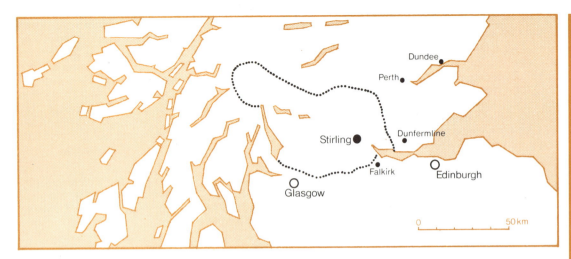

Fig. 7:3 The general retail and service hinterland of Stirling.

each baker, according to Davies would be 1/50. To simplify the calculations we multiply by 100 to give $1/50 \times 100 = 2$.

By counting the total number of establishments of each type in the study area a centrality value can be calculated for each function. If there were 10 banks the centrality value for a bank would be $1/10 \times 100$ or 10. For each settlement the total centrality value can then be counted by adding up the scores for each function. Assume that a grocer has a centrality value in the study area of 1, a chemist 8, a doctor 20 and a post office 6. Then a village in that study area with a post office (6), two grocers (1×2), a chemist (8), a doctor (20) and a baker (2) would have a total centrality value of $6 + 2 + 8 + 20 + 2 = 38$. We can then compare the centrality scores of the different settlements to see if a hierarchy of Central Places can be identified.

We could also plot on a graph the centrality score for a settlement against the population size of the settlement (see Fig. 7:5). If there is a relationship between total centrality scores and population size it should be identifiable on the graph. A perfect positive correlation would produce a straight line as shown in Fig. 7:6. This would mean that total centrality scores increase in exact proportion to the population of settlements. The total centrality score for a settlement is often called the **Functional Index**.

Urban Land Use

Successful studies of urban land use depend upon two basic features. First, there must be clear aims for the study and not simply a massive collection of facts. Second, land-use mapping requires a well-constructed classification. A general survey of all types of land use could group the different types under three broad headings; townscape, farmscape, wildscape. The location of each category could be analysed and related to factors altitude. However, this grouping is not very appropriate for an urban study because most land uses would be listed under one heading, townscape.

If all types of land use are to be examined, the classification should identify various principal groups, e.g. retail, services, industry, warehouses, residential, transport, entertainment and recreation, public buildings, offices, green space,

Fig. 7:4
Standard Industrial Classification listing of types of retail uses.

Grocers
Grocers with off-licence
Grocers with bakery goods

Dairymen
Butchers
Fishmongers, Poulterers
Greengrocers, Fruiterers
Greengrocers, Fruiterers selling Fish
Bread and Flour Confectioners
Off-licence
Other Food Shops

Confectioners, Tobacconists, Newsagents

Boot and Shoe shops
Men's Outwear shops
Other Men's wear shops
Women's Outwear shops
Other Women's wear, Drapery and General clothing shops

Domestic Furniture shops
Soft Furnishings
Antique Dealers
Second Hand Furniture
Art Dealers and Picture Framers
Radio and Electrical Goods
Radio and T.V. Hire
Radio and Electrical goods with Repairs
Electrical goods with Contractors
Cycles, Cycles and Motor Accessories

Radio and Cycle
Pram
Ironmongers and Hardware

China and Hardware

Wall paper and paint
Booksellers, Stationers

Second hand books
Circulating libraries
Dispensing Chemist
Other retailers of Chemist goods
Photographic goods
Jewellery, Watch and Clock Repairs
Leather goods
Sports goods
Toys
Fancy goods
Florists
Nurserymen, Garden seedsmen
Pet and pet foods
Pawnbrokers
General Second Hand Dealers
Sub Post Offices with minor retail sales

Other Non-Food Shops

Department Stores
Variety Stores
Other General Stores
Electricity Showrooms
Gas Showrooms

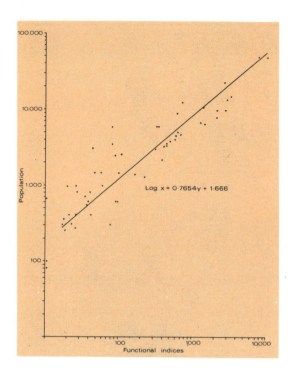

Fig. 7:5 *Correlation between the functional index and the population size of settlements in Ayrshire.*

$Log x = 0.7654y + 1.666$

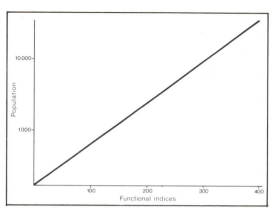

Fig. 7:6 *Perfect correlation between the functional index and the population size of settlements.*

Offices				Flats	Flats
Offices				Flats	Flats
Offices				Flats	Flats
Offices	Department Store	Hotel		Flats	Flats
Offices			Offices	Flats
Shop			Offices	Flats
Shop			Offices	Shop
			Shop	Shop

Fig. 7:7 *The vertical dimension of land use.*

derelict land, farmland and water areas. Each principal group would also have sub-types. Residences could be grouped into house-types (detached, terraced, flats, maisonettes, cottages) and tenure categories (owner-occupied, rented from private landlord, rented from local authority). Very detailed classifications exist such as the Standard Industrial Classification (S.I.C.) used in the British Census of Distribution. Fig. 7:4 lists the types of retail land use recognized in S.I.C. (1971). However, retail changes can occur. For example the classification did not recognize supermarkets or freezer suppliers as specific types, although they could be classified under the heading of other food shops. This is a detailed classification of types of shops because it was intended for a study of that function.

In an individual research project a practical solution to the problem of classification is to use a system of major classes and then note sub-types within each class as they are encountered in the field. Unless you study the city centre or a shopping district there would only be a relatively small number of shops within most urban transects. A workable classification might distinguish convenience and comparison shops as two major groups and then record actual shops in detail in the field survey. However, a group project, in which a large part of a town or city is to be mapped by adding together the work of each individual, must have everyone using the same classification. This will ensure that comparable maps and results can be achieved.

Once the hypotheses have been stated and the classification decided, the mapping and recording is the final stage of the fieldwork. Large scale Ordnance Survey plans (1:10650 or 1:2500) which show the pattern of plots simplify the mapping of land use. Care must be taken to cover the whole area under investigation including side-streets and minor lanes. One complication involves the vertical aspect of land use. Most buildings consist of more than one storey or level. When the type of use is the same on all levels, as in office blocks or multi-storey blocks of flats, there is only the simple task of noting the number of floors of that use on that plot. But there are many buildings, especially those in shopping areas, where a change of use occurs within the building as we move upwards from the ground floor. One

solution is to construct two fieldmaps: one of ground floor use and the other of the use above the ground floor. An alternative is to draw sections in your field notebook of each street frontage and record the actual use of each floor (see Fig. 7:7). Diagrams, graphs and tables of percentage of various land uses can then be compiled to illustrate the results. In a general land-use survey possible topics for investigation are the relationships between land use and the distance from the city centre or from major transport routes. We could suggest that as the distance increases so the intensity of land use would decrease. You could use ideas developed in Chapter 4 such as the bid-rent curve.

When a more specific topic is under examination, the hypotheses will depend upon the nature of the area and of the topic. For example, in the city centre, you might be interested in the pattern of land use. You could suggest that different types of land use will occur at different locations and that the pattern will relate to land values. The latter can be measured by information recorded in the Valuation Roll which is kept in the Assessor's Department of the local authority. An alternative method might be to count pedestrian traffic flows at various points within the centre. The argument supporting this method is that pedestrian flows in the centre of a city are a guide to the intensity of shopping activity. Therefore, they give an indirect measure of the attractiveness of different locations. However, whilst shops attract customers, much of the business of offices

121

may be by post or telephone. Pedestrian flows may be of little assistance, therefore, in distinguishing between various non-shopping areas, e.g. between offices and warehouses.

Another specific land-use study could involve the mapping of a particular use, e.g. housing or derelict land or recreational space. The location pattern could then be analysed using the ideas of clustering and random distribution and by relating the distribution to other phenomena, e.g. transport routes, the city centre, etc.

When detailed large-scale maps are not available it may be necessary to add areal measurements by pacing out the length of the frontage of buildings. Equally sketches of particular townscapes, distinctive sections of land use, may be a useful means of recording visual images of areas. When studying residential areas it is always useful to record comparatively minor aspects of the urban environment such as the location of telephone kiosks, street crossings, bus stops and post boxes. This provides a record of additional amenities which may be of relevance in analysing or explaining patterns and permits certain hypotheses to be tested, e.g. the topic of **hazard zones** in residential environments. Many of these topics may require other supplementary information from pedestrian or traffic surveys or from questionnaire studies of a random sample of residents or interviews with particular specialists, e.g. police, local authority roads department officials, etc. Use the field notebook to record important points of detail such as yellow lines and other parking restrictions, the means of service access to shops for delivery and refuse removal or the size and nature of gardens and of formal open space and play areas in residential areas. By these means vital flesh can be added to the skeleton of the land-use map. It also serves to extend the array of different topics which can be studied.

Perception, Attitudes and Behaviour

Studies of perception, attitudes and behaviour involve questionnaires. A random or stratified sample must be used to eliminate bias. Questions should be carefully worded to avoid ambiguity or vagueness and to avoid leading the respondent towards a particular reply. Examples of

behavioural topics are shopping, journey-to-work, recreational activities, local area activities such as clubs and associations. Apart from questions about the specific topic, other standard questions such as the age and occupation of the respondent may provide valuable information which can be used to explain behavioural patterns.

The questionnaire should provide a realistic picture of complex situations. For example, in a study of shoppers, a question about the reason for shopping at a particular centre must recognize the possibility of multi-purpose trips. By this we mean that shopping may be only one of several reasons for a journey. The trip may involve, for example, an appointment with a doctor or dentist or a visit to relatives and friends. In the study of perception and of attitudes it is particularly important that questions are very carefully worded.

Many studies have shown that as distance increases perceptions become less accurate. A simple test of this hypothesis would be to ask a random sample of people the distance to various places in the country. We should expect the greatest accuracy to occur for nearby locations and inaccuracy generally to increase with distance from the location of the sample. One such study was conducted recently in Stirling and the results did confirm this notion of distance decay. The accuracy percentage (within 5 km.) for places within a 50 km. radius of Stirling was 82 per cent; up to 100 km. the percentage decreased to 71 per cent and distances over 150 km. achieved only 61 per cent accuracy. Apart from testing the accuracy of geographical knowledge we may be interested in the perceptions which people have of particular areas or settlements or shopping centres. Normally this research involves the use of a scale ranging from positive reactions (like) to negative attitudes (dislike). It may be possible to relate the perceptions to behaviour but this is not often possible within the same sample survey. Common products of these studies are maps of areal desirability such as those shown in Figs. 7:8 and 7:9.

Samples of school leavers in Liverpool and Bristol

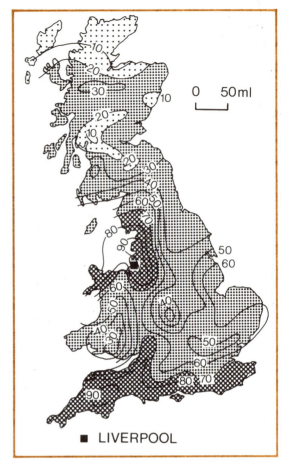

Fig. 7:8 *Liverpool school pupils' views of the desirability of various areas of Britain (P. GOULD and R. WHITE).*

were asked to rank distinct parts of Britain in terms of residential desirability. In general a distance decay relationship is identifiable, i.e. the area closest to Liverpool in Fig. 7:8 or Bristol Fig. 7:9 was rated quite highly. However, the overall relationship was imperfect. People had more knowledge of some areas than others but this was not solely a function of distance from their own locality. Some areas feature prominently on television or in newspapers. Notice

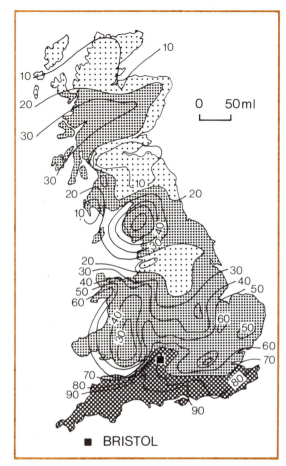

Fig. 7:9 Bristol school pupils' views of the desirability of various areas of Britain (P. GOULD and R. WHITE).

■ BRISTOL

prominently featured on national television or in newspaper coverage. Unless you live there you will have limited information, positive or negative, about these areas.

Assignment

1 Is it possible to project an image? Examine brochures of holiday resorts, industrial estates and shopping centres. List the points in the brochures which project a perception of that area or feature. How could you devise a means of testing the accuracy of the image by **(a)** visiting **(b)** without visiting, the area?

A major problem in the study of attitudes is that the respondents are often placed in a hypothetical or game situation. For example, if we are studying attitudes about residential areas and housing environments, questions about the type of houses people would like to occupy or the location of the housing are hypothetical in the sense that the respondent is probably not thinking of moving in the near future. It is important that in this type of study you should decide whether you want people to answer with no restraints (e.g. ability to pay) or if you want to seek a realistic choice if they were to move house in the near future.

It is often easier to conduct a survey of attitudes when there is a clear focus such as reactions to a proposed road, airport, shopping development or school closure. This does not imply that other studies of attitudes are less valid but merely that respondents may relate more readily to the topic. It is probably quite unrealistic to assume that everyone has carefully worked out their attitudes to every aspect of geography, society, economics, etc. You should bear these points in mind when selecting a project.

Data Sources

The Chapter has emphasized field surveys but a considerable amount of research can be based upon data which has been collected by government and other bodies and institutions. The use of this form of information may save time which can then be devoted to the analysis of the data. In addition, data stored in libraries or other collections should be consulted to provide background information about the area or topic or to support results from fieldwork.

Data sources vary in character and location. It is often essential to use a comprehensive source. In the National Census, for example, information is gathered from every household and tabulated by various areas, e.g. wards, parishes, towns, regions and counties. The advantages of this sort of information are that it is collected in a standard way for every household in the country. By comparison, some data sources are very incomplete. For example, the publication *Who's Who* lists information about certain people, normally important people in the arts, business, politics and public life, but it is a selection and is not comprehensive.

Another important point is the question of accessibility of the data. Major public libraries will keep a wide selection of information about the local area ranging from a selection of Ordnance Survey maps at various scales to Census volumes. Access is comparatively simple and many libraries have a section specializing on the local area. The staff in charge of these collections can give valuable assistance in your search for information. Various departments of large local authorities are massive collectors of data about the area, e.g. housing, transport and industrial information. However, the material is not necessarily on open access for public inspection although it may be used for research by prior arrangement and approval of the appropriate council. Equally, national government is a major source of data, especially through HMSO publications. Fortunately, many government reports are available in major public libraries.

The following data sources are available in libraries in most major towns and cities. Some will be available in local libraries and in schools.

PHOTOGRAPHS

The chief use of vertical or oblique aerial photographs is the recognition of geographical features, especially types of land use. Colour photographs are available but expense will probably mean that you use black and white photographs. For agricultural land use colour is of considerable assistance but with experience it is possible to

both sets of school leavers rated highly holiday areas in South-West England and Southern England. They had a favourable perception of these areas. Respondents in Bristol thought that the Lake District would offer an attractive residential environment but they did not consider the industrial area of Lancashire to be attractive. Liverpool respondents, however, with better local knowledge, rated some of these areas quite highly. Equally, some areas of Britain are not normally distinguish between cereal crops and grass on black and white photographs. This source can provide a valuable plan of settlement and suggest possible spatial relationships which could then be examined in the field.

Photographs provide information about:

1. The shape and form of settlements, or parts of settlements
2. The layout of farm buildings and fields
3. Functional areas and land use
4. Growth of settlement, by style and age of buildings
5. Site and situation
6. Possible problems such as pollution (spoil heaps), congestion (contorted road network), decay (dense housing patterns and areas of derelict space within urban centres)
7. Solutions to problems such as the planned layout of housing areas, parks and planned recreational space
8. Competition between land uses, shown by very different uses being situated close to each other, e.g. hospital and farmland or scrapyard and farmland.

Remember that photographs are taken from various directions and heights. North is not necessarily at the top of the photograph. An overlapping pair of vertical photographs gives considerable information when studied with the use of a stereoscope. This gives a three-dimensional image and assists in the identification of land use, e.g. number of storeys of buildings.

MAPS

Numerous maps are published in a variety of styles at different scales and relating to many topics. All schools will have a selection of Ordnance Survey maps. The 1:50 000 sheets use several colours. They provide basic locational information and can be a means of supplementing and supporting the interpretation of photographs. In general, as the scale of O.S. plans increases, the use of colour decreases. Thus large-scale plans are confined to black, grey and white. These plans (e.g. 25 inch or 1:2500) give detailed information such as the location of plot boundaries and individual buildings which is invaluable in the study of the land use of a set-

tlement or a part of a settlement. The 1:10 000 or 1:10 560 maps are especially useful when an area of several square kilometres is to be studied. A larger scale (e.g. 1:1250) would require several sheets whilst a smaller scale would mean the loss of detailed information.

Similar information to that listed for photographs can be gained from map analysis. Large-scale plans (1:2500 or 1:1250) provide quite a lot of land-use information including the recording of named urban functions. Map analysis of rural land use is more complex. At the 1:50 000 scale the area can be divided into zones of townscape, farmscape and wildscape. Within the farmscape category further divisions can be suggested on the basis of altitude, slope and drainage, information recorded on the map and because of specific symbols relating to marsh or woodland. Larger scale maps provide additional information on field patterns and drainage but it is desirable to consult specialized maps such as soil maps, climatic maps, and those of the Second Land Utilization Survey of Great Britain.

Other specialized maps include the Goad plans of town and city centres in Britain and the Geographia plans of land use in major urban areas. The coloured Geographia plans provide a source of the general pattern of land use which may suggest hypotheses for further research, e.g. concerning the location of shopping centres. The Goad plans record the name of the use on each plot and are very useful in studies of the city centre.

Remember to check the date of a map. It may have been surveyed more than a decade ago and changes will have occurred since the survey. Always check the accuracy during the subsequent field study. If no field study is to be undertaken only use recent maps, surveyed within the past six years, if you suspect that changes will have occurred, e.g. a city experiencing redevelopment or a rural area in which the agricultural patterns have altered (livestock to crops or vice versa). Old maps are invaluable in studies of change, e.g. comparison of settlement at the start of the twentieth century and today.

STATISTICS

Detailed agricultural statistics for parishes in

England and Wales are available from the Ministry of Agriculture Records Office. This information is collated from an annual agricultural survey which farmers are required to complete. There are differences in the data available for Scotland but information can be obtained from the appropriate section of the Scottish Office in Edinburgh.

National and local government publications provide a mass of statistics relating to aspects of the social and economic geography of settlements. Apart from the decennial Census in Britain, the most recent being the 1981 Census, Government publications include the General Household Survey, the Family Expenditure Survey and the Earnings Survey. The annual report of the General Household Survey, based on a sample of 15 000 households, covers the topics of housing, migration, employment, education, health and health services and fertility. It is a useful source of broad comparative data, but of limited value for detailed local studies. The same comments apply to the other general surveys including publications such as the Abstract of British Labour Statistics.

Rather than hunt in a haphazard fashion you should consult a guide to the sources such as the Guide to Official Statistics which lists all government publications and also those of professional organizations and institutes.

The National Census is a major data source in geography. It contains information at various areal scales from small areas (a few hundred households) to major regions (millions of people). The information relates to demographic characteristics (age, sex, size of family, etc.) and various social and economic features (housing tenure, house size and amenities, occupation, education, etc.). The material can be used to examine areal patterns and specific relationships, e.g. type of housing and social and economic characteristics of occupants. The reports analyse migration in the period between each Census. The data is also classified by age of person so that particular groups can be studied, e.g. pensioners.

In addition to the Census the Registrar-General issues annual reports about the population with particular reference to births, deaths, migration and health.

Apart from the Voters' Roll and the Valuation Roll there are few standardized local data sources which are always available for public inspection. The Voters' Roll is a handy source for compiling a random sample since households are listed in an ordered manner. Some large authorities, such as the Greater London Council, publish an annual abstract of statistics, but this is not a widespread practice.

One major source of information is the numerous planning reports of local authorities and other public bodies, e.g. Transport Executives or Airport Authorities. These should be handled with greater care. You must distinguish between any survey material and the planning proposals. Never assume that because planning proposals were made some time ago they will now be in existence as buildings or land uses. There is often a substantial time-lag before proposals are implemented. Moreover, some proposals are never implemented. The scheme may be abandoned due to rising costs or changes in the projected demand, e.g. fall in birth rate. Even when the proposals are carried out, there may be changes, sometimes of a substantial nature, between the original plan and the final development. One possible topic for a field study would be the investigation of this situation by comparing the proposals with the results of a field survey.

OTHER SOURCES

Numerous further sources can be of considerable value. For example, *Yellow Pages* and Kelly's *Directories*, both of which list functions such as shops and services, provide a simple source of information for a study concerned with ranking various settlements in terms of service provision. The data is incomplete but the omissions will primarily relate to smaller enterprises which should not seriously disrupt the results. Social information can be obtained from *Who's Who*, *Who Owns Whom* and *Who Was Who*.

Newspapers can be a useful source of local information particularly concerning developments and any controversy surrounding them.

Finally, there may be valuable local or regional material which is relevant to your proposed study. It is impossible to give more precise information about such material other than to offer the advice that you consult the local librarian or the chief executive's office of the local authority. New Towns, for example, are image-conscious and produce a substantial amount of general and detailed data on a fairly regular basis. Elsewhere most authorities produce occasional information on specific topics (housing or transport) and on projects.

This section on data sources has primarily assumed access to British sources. However, most general points apply in any setting. All countries conduct an occasional Census of Population. Equally they all have a variety of data sources ranging from a national map coverage, at some scale, to local reports and surveys.

Whatever the data sources used, you must become familiar with the character of that information. For example, if it is a map — what is shown and what is not recorded? What is the contour interval? When was the map surveyed? What do the symbols mean?

Before starting a project you should read the Introduction to this chapter and check your plan to ensure that each stage has been organized satisfactorily. Space does not permit a section on techniques of analysis. You should refer to Chapter 5 in *Urban Geography* by Gordon and Dick or to other books such as P. Toyne and P. Newby *Techniques in Human Geography*; R. G. Woodcock and M. J. Bailey *Quantitative Geography*; and J. R. Short *Urban Data Sources*.

INDEX

(Author's names are capitalized)